Also by Rosemary Sprague

ROSEMARY SPRAGUE

Chilton Book Company

Philadelphia   New York   London

"... nor till the poets among us ... can present
for inspection,
'imaginary gardens with real toads in them. ...'"

MARIANNE MOORE

IMAGINARY

GARDENS

A Study of Five American Poets

SAN MATEO PUBLIC LIBRARY, SAN MATEO, CALIFORNIA

COPYRIGHT ACKNOWLEDGMENTS

Emily Dickinson

Reprinted by permission of the publishers and the Trustees of Amherst College from Thomas H. Johnson, Editor, THE POEMS OF EMILY DICKINSON, Cambridge, Mass.: The Belknap Press of Harvard University, Copyright, 1951, 1955, by The President and Fellows of Harvard College.

Also by permission of Little, Brown & Company (Inc.) Copyright 1929, © 1957 by Mary L. Hampson. Copyright 1935 by Martha Dickinson Bianchi, © Renewed 1963 by Mary L. Hampson. Copyright 1914, 1942 by Martha Dickinson Bianchi.

Reprinted by permission of the publishers from THE LETTERS OF EMILY DICKINSON edited by Thomas H. Johnson, Cambridge, Mass.: Harvard University Press, Copyright 1958, by The President and Fellows of Harvard College.

Amy Lowell

Reprinted from SWORD BLADES AND POPPY SEEDS by Amy Lowell, JOHN KEATS by Amy Lowell, A DOME OF MANY COLOURED GLASS by Amy Lowell, A CRITICAL FABLE by Amy Lowell and AMY LOWELL: A CHRONICLE by S. Foster Damon by permission of Houghton Mifflin Company.

To quote from Amy Lowell manuscript material in The Houghton Library, Harvard University, by permission of the Harvard College Library, and from the Amy Lowell Trustees.

for Arthur Franklin White

Poet, Professor, and Friend

Contents

Foreword

I began *Imaginary Gardens* knowing that it would be a challenge. Writing of five poets, all of whom have achieved recognition in the past seventy years, has posed certain unique problems not encountered when considering those whom a century or more has guaranteed their place in the literary pantheon. Contemporary assessments, however, do have a certain value, and this book has proved to be a veritable *voyage en Serendip*. Because published criticism concerning these five remarkable women is so varying in quantity and quality—about Emily Dickinson almost too much has been written; about Marianne Moore much more remains to be written; while Amy Lowell, Sara Teasdale, and Edna St. Vincent Millay have been comparatively neglected during the past decade—I have followed my usual procedure in avoiding the critics as much as possible. My purpose has been to permit each poet to tell her story in her own words, through her poetry, letters, and published statements, and supplement these with the recollections of those who knew her and have been kind enough to share those recollections with me.

A book such as this does not spring into being full grown, like Athena from the head of Zeus. The influences which shaped it came into being long before pen was put to paper. Had my parents not read and recited poems to me long before I learned to talk, much less read, and had volumes of poetry not been on our library shelves, it is doubtful that I ever would have learned that poetry is important. Their residence in St. Louis, Sara Teasdale's birthplace, during the first years of their marriage, about which they told me much, has been of inestimable help in recreating that poet's girlhood ambiance. My mother grew up in Chicago, and has been able to supply considerable firsthand information about Harriet Monroe and the midwest poetry renaissance. Finally, my dear father and mother sent me to Bryn Mawr, where—among other incalculable gains—I had the unforgettable experience of hearing Edna St. Vincent Millay read her poetry, and the opportunity to read for myself the work of one of my alma mater's most illustrious alumnae, Marianne Moore. Certainly, under influences, I must also credit my own New England ancestry, and the annual summer safaris to that part of the country where—as part education and cultural enlightenment—I was taken to visit museums, libraries, and all the major "literary shrines." Little did I know at the time that what I was experiencing as a genuine pleasure would ultimately prove to be so useful!

Two friends no longer on this earth have also contributed enormously to my knowledge and understanding, though I did not realize the extent of that contribution until I began work on *Imaginary Gardens.* The late Everett Shinn conversed with me on several occasions about his early years in New York; his perceptive painter's eye had noted every detail, and he translated his memories of Greenwich Village into equally vivid, expressive language. I have used my notes of those conversations in the chapter on Edna St. Vincent Millay. To Oscar Williams I owe my first real introduction to contemporary poetry; his critical sense and knowledge of literary tradition were exceeded only by his own poetic gift, and his lectures, letters, and conversations have given me information and insight obtainable in no other way. I have drawn on these freely, as I am certain he would have wished.

For the actual writing of *Imaginary Gardens,* the usual acknowledgments of "permissions to quote" cannot begin to repay my indebtedness. I owe much to my editor, John Marion, for asking me to undertake the book in the first place, and for encouraging me through all the usual—and some unusual!—creative vicissitudes. I must thank Charles Butler, director of Lancaster Library, Longwood College, for his prompt, unquestioning response to requests for books on inter-library loan; and the staff of the Virginia State Library at Richmond for bibliographical assistance. For the chapter on Emily Dickinson, I am grateful to Professor Thomas H. Johnson for having written his *Emily Dickinson, An Interpretive Biography,* which I frequently consulted for biographical details; and to my friend and colleague, Professor William J. Sowder of Longwood College, for some valuable insights into her poetry.

Professor S. Foster Damon's remarkably fine biography of Amy Lowell is the chief source of information about her life, and I have followed it in writing the biographical section of my essay about her. The staff of Houghton Library, Harvard University, provided most courteous assistance when I arrived on a hot July day to work on the Amy Lowell manuscripts, and I am especially appreciative of the kindness of Mr. W. L. Bond for helping me to obtain a photograph of the Putnam portrait of Amy Lowell. The permission of the trustees of the Amy Lowell estate, Messers G. d'Andelot Bellin and Conrad W. Obendorfer, to quote from her manuscripts is also most gratefully acknowledged.

The chapter on Sara Teasdale could not have been written without the generosity of two of her friends, Miss Margery Mansfield and Mr. John Hall Wheelock, both of whom, through correspondence and conversation, gave me valuable information about her life and poetry. I am also very grateful to Miss Margaret Conklin, literary executor of the estate of Sara Teasdale, for her kind and knowledgable assistance in a variety of ways, and especially for her permission to quote from Miss Teasdale's unpublished biography of Christina Rossetti. I wish also to thank Professor A. Bartlett Giamatti of Yale University, for permission to quote from one of his lectures.

Mrs. Norma Millay Ellis must receive special thanks for her graciousness in reading and approving the section concerning her sister and for her permission to use excerpts from her sister's poems and letters, as must Mr. Edmund Wilson for allowing me to quote from one of his essays. I am also grateful to Mrs. Miriam Gurko for her splendid biography of Edna

St. Vincent Millay, *Restless Spirit*, which I followed in writing the biographical section of my essay, and to Miss Elizabeth Riley of Crowell Publishers for permission to quote therefrom.

Finally, my wholehearted, unbounded appreciation goes to Miss Marianne Moore, for her kindness in sharing with me her endlessly fascinating mind and gentle heart. Especially do I wish to thank this great lady, who is presently engaged in writing her own memoir, for so generously helping me to write about her, and for reading and approving what I have written.

Rosemary Sprague

May 26, 1969

Emily Dickinson

1830-1886

OF all major American poets, none has been subjected to more industrious scrutiny by critics and biographers than Emily Dickinson. Born on December 10, 1830, she lived the greater part of her life in the seclusion of her father's home in Amherst, Massachusetts. But from the moment that her first volume of poetry, published posthumously in 1890, made its sensationally successful appearance, this shy New England woman became the focus of a fascinated interest which has continued unabated into this century. Her simple lyrics, dealing with the commonplaces of the daily life she experienced, yet shot through with brilliant insight and a religious exaltation that verges at times on genuine mysticism, have profoundly influenced all the poets who came after her. Indeed, as the late Oscar Williams once remarked, "She was like John Donne, in a way. Poetry was never the same, after her. It couldn't be." Biographers, tantalized by the hints of an unrequited love affair which drove her into becoming a recluse, have written volumes in an attempt to identify the mysterious man in her life; and psychologists, professional and amateur, have saddled her with an Electra complex in explanation for her never marrying. But despite all their efforts, the real Emily Dickinson continued to elude her pursuers with the serenity that her freely chosen mode of life brought to her "loosened spirit," soaring high above the New England meadows like the larks that she so loved. Perhaps the essential clue to her remarkable personality is to be found in her own words: "To live is so startling, it leaves but little time for other occupations." [1]

For it must be admitted unequivocally that Emily Dickinson truly "lived," if to live means to experience, endure, and enjoy spiritually, intellectually, and emotionally all that life sends; but her life was startling in its lack of outward activity. Only five times did she leave Amherst at all; once to visit an aunt in Boston; a second time when she went as a student to Mt. Holyoke; again when she and her sister Lavinia visited Washington during her father's term in the House of Representatives; and, finally, on two separate occasions when she spent several months in Boston, undergoing treatment for an eye condition brought on by excessive reading and writing. Otherwise, she remained at home, usually inaccessible to casual visitors, and, during the last ten years of her life, even to close friends. The white-gowned figure of "Miss Emily," glimpsed occasionally at an open window or through a space in the tall evergreen hedge that surrounded her garden, is Amherst legend. Only children actually spoke with her, and they received cookies and flowers at her hands. The outside world knew her through the letters which poured unceasingly from her pen, and neighbors and townspeople by the little poems that accompanied gifts of jelly or hot bread—poems that frequently puzzled more than amused the recipients.

But in her hopes and dreams, her inner life was marked by an intensity that still, a century later, is communicated through her poems with all the vividness of her own immediate reactions. She knew love, both the joy of it and its grief. She knew the meaning of both rejection and renunciation. She hammered at the gates of Eternity to find the answer to the imponderable fact of death. She knew the happiness of deep friendship and all the anguish that betrayal could bring. Beneath the serene facade that her daguerreotype portrays, with her russet hair drawn smoothly into a chignon at the nape of her neck, the high forehead, the wide-set brown eyes, the generous mouth and dimpled chin, was tumult as well as simplicity. Emily Dickinson knew all the torment and ecstasy of a person committed to know all there was to experience. There was no need for her to *find* a life. She found it where she was. Her own words best express what she believed: "I find ecstasy in living—the mere sense of living is joy enough." [2] Yet there is restraint in her ecstasy; she was not one for excess, as her sharply pruned verse

reveals. And over and above all else, there is that oblique—
sometimes rueful—overtone that permeates much of her writing, which can be attributed to the fact that she was cognizant
of the quality of her special vocation: "My business is to love." [3]

She is the more remarkable because, so far as can be ascer-
tained, there is nothing in her family heritage to explain her.
Unlike the Lowells, the Dickinsons had never been a literary
family—quite the contrary. The original ancestor, Nathaniel
Dickinson, British yeoman in his native country, had come to
Massachusetts during the early seventeenth century Puritan
exodus from England, and, by all accounts, had brought sterling
qualities of character and ability to the new world. He became
a deacon of the Congregational Church, and was chosen recorder
for the town of Hadley before his death in 1676. His great-
grandson, Nathan, had moved his family in 1743 to the location
which became the town of Amherst, and Nathan's great-grand-
son, Samuel Fowler, put the Dickinson stamp on the embryo
town which would hold for three successive generations. Samuel
Fowler Dickinson, Emily's grandfather, was a typical, substantial post-Revolutionary War American—a pillar of the church
and devoted to the increase of education. Believing that even
his own education at Dartmouth College had been too inadequate, he devoted much of his ample means and all the time
he could conscientiously spare from his flourishing law practice
and his duties as town clerk to the improvement of Massachusetts schools. He was the leader in the founding of Amherst
Academy in 1814; and hardly had it opened its doors to students
before he formed another committee for the founding of "The
Collegiate Institution," later to become Amherst College. As
was true with every college founded in the United States at that
time, Amherst was first and foremost dedicated to the theological education of young men for the ministry, but the curriculum
included *belles lettres*, music, and science as well. Thus, Emily
Dickinson, because of her remarkable family heritage, came by
her love of literature and her craving for knowledge quite naturally. One might say that it was inborn.

Samuel Fowler's son, Edward—Emily's father—followed in his own father's footsteps. He studied at Amherst Academy, went for two years to Yale, then returned for his junior year to the Collegiate Institution. But the new college had not yet received its charter, and, with that prudence which was to be characteristic of his entire life, he decided that he must not risk a possibly unaccredited degree. So he returned to Yale, graduating in 1823, studied law and worked in his father's office, and, in 1826, hung out his own shingle. Very quickly he became one of the political leaders of Amherst, serving in both the Massachusetts legislature and senate, later, as a member of the Congress. From 1835 to 1873 he was treasurer of Amherst College, and helped materially to guide it through all the difficulties a college usually experiences in its early years. He was also substantially involved in bringing the railroad to the town—a feat in 1853 analagous to the establishment of an airport in the twentieth century. He occupied a position of enormous power in the community, but he was greatly respected because he never misused it. He was a man of whom it was said that he was "as good as his word," and in early New England there could be no higher praise.

Emily, then, lived in the kind of environment that such a father provided. That Edward Dickinson ruled his household with a firm hand is undoubted. But in so doing, he was only fulfilling the duty expected of the head of such a household. His marriage to Miss Emily Norcross of Monson had been based on deepest affection, as the letters he wrote to her during their courtship plainly indicate, but practicality and suitability, as well as pride and admiration, would have entered his consideration as well. His wife was a "good manager," devout, unassuming, never known to contradict or disagree with her husband, and content with the domesticity for which she had been prepared; though she had received advanced education at a finishing school in New Haven, she was not especially interested in intellectual or political concerns beyond the boundaries of their home. "My mother does not care for thought," [4] Emily wrote of her, and it was doubtless this attitude towards the world which led her eldest daughter to question rather wistfully, "I suppose a mother is one to whom you hurry when you are troubled." [5]

In justice to Mrs. Dickinson, however, Emily's troubles usually stemmed from spiritual and intellectual sources, and would have been difficult for a woman like herself to understand. And Emily's youthful impatience did not further much understanding or tolerance. These did come with maturity as Emily grew in compassion and insight; her mother's death in 1882, after a long illness through which Emily nursed her devotedly, "stunned [her] spirit." [6]

It was "Papa" who was the profound influence in shaping his eldest daughter's life, for, of his three children, she most resembled him in appearance and character. (It should be noted that Mr. Dickinson was not lacking in what the French call *esprit*—he drove the most spirited horse in town, and once impatiently rang the church bells to call the town's attention to the beauty of a particularly magnificent sunset which they were ignoring for more ordinary, prosaic pursuits.)

His son, William Austin (usually called "Austin"), had inherited more of his mother's gentle disposition than of his father's decisiveness. Lavinia, the youngest child, was more typical of the average girl of her time, interested in marriage, parties, flirtations, and clothes.

Emily adored her brother, who seems to have understood her best of the entire family, though not to the point of agreeing with her when their ideas or opinions clashed. She was devoted to her sister, and she gave her mother dutiful affection. But her father was foremost in her love, and she, apparently, was his favorite. He bought her the books she asked for, even while he urged her not to tire her eyes by reading them, and he seems not to have been overly perturbed by her frequent absences from school because of recurrent ill health. He sent her to the Academy for her education; he indulged her wish for her own piano and piano lessons, and permitted her to attend singing school.

She assisted at receptions that her parents gave for the trustees, faculty and students of Amherst. Her early letters are a delightful melange of Latin, history, botany, sewing, gardening, and bread-baking, for her education also included doing household tasks. Women might be educated, but they were not excused from fulfilling their home duties on that account. In 1847, when Emily went to South Hadley Seminary (which later became Mt. Holyoke College), she studied chemistry, physiology, and algebra, and she was also required to "keep her room," and to wash and dry the table knives after every meal.

Apart from her brilliant intellect, which would invariably set her apart, there was little on the surface to differentiate Emily from other girls. She was not as pretty nor as obviously gay as, for instance, her own sister Lavinia, but she could and did enjoy a good time. She possessed a considerable wit which sparkled in conversation and in the Valentine verses that she composed every year for her friends. She apparently felt no concern about her future, nor was there any apparent need. Papa and brother Austin would always see that she was well taken care of, and, fortunately, she loved her home.

Emily's letters to Abiah Root, her closest friend, however, reveal an inner turmoil. In 1846 she had just passed her fifteenth year and, in recognition of this feminine "adult" status, she had put up her hair. At this moment in her life, she was expected to think seriously about her religious commitment, and, though she had gone to Sunday School all her life, she was supposed to experience a "conversion" and join the church. No doubt her mother was most influential in wanting Emily to do this; for a child, especially a girl of that day, raised in a good Christian home to follow any other procedure would be unthinkable. It is true that Edward Dickinson had not yet formally joined the church in 1846, and would not do so until 1850, but his procrastination was motivated by a genuine matter of conscience, not by what was termed unprincipled neglect. Emily herself agonized over this decision in a manner that, for a fifteen-year-old girl, seems almost unbelievable to eyes reading her letters a century later, but which was quite normal in nineteenth-century

New England. ". . . I never enjoyed such perfect peace and happiness as in the short time in which I felt I had found my Saviour," she mourned to Abiah. "But I soon forgot my morning prayer, or else it was irksome to me. One by one my old habits returned, and I cared less for religion than ever." [7]

Friends prayed over her and reasoned with her, but to no avail. During her year at Mt. Holyoke she was under constant pressure to make her formal commitment, but the end of the term found her still among the "obdurate ones," and, for this reason, in a very real sense isolated from those who had "cast their burdens on Christ."

"All, all are kind to me, but their tones fall strangely on my ears, and their countenances meet mine not like home faces. . . ." [8] she wrote to Abiah. At least in Amherst she could depend upon her family's love if not their complete understanding; *they* would never make her feel like an outsider, even if they disapproved. Also, she felt a deep regret at her inability to become the kind of Christian that she honestly wished to be; ". . . it is hard for me to give up the world." [9] She loved life too much, and the stern evangelical counsels, which demanded that she regard the most innocent pleasures as certain roads to damnation, she found too grim, too severe. She could not conscientiously bring herself to take such a step, and what she could not do genuinely, she would not do at all. A time would come when she would willingly renounce the world, but she would take this action in full awareness of the sacrifice she was making, counting the cost in gain, as well as loss.

Meanwhile, she was censured for her obstinacy, but, having made her decision, she learned quickly how to reply to criticism. "*God* is sitting here, looking into my very soul, to see if I think the right th'ots," she wrote to Abiah.

Yet I am not afraid, for I try to be right and good, and he knows everyone of my struggles. He looks very gloriously, and everything bright seems dull beside him, and I don't dare look directly at him for fear I shall die.[10]

Formal, institutionalized expression of faith could hold no possible attraction for one who experienced the actual presence of God like a confident child. On the other hand, she also enjoyed the daring that such a course enjoined upon her. To her friend's continual remonstrances, she replied, "The shore is safer, Abiah, but I love to buffet the sea . . . oh, I love the danger!" [11] She was one of the few women of her time who, it would seem, was destined to find her own way, and neither family nor friends could help her in her quest.

It is impossible to overestimate the effect that this religious turmoil had upon her, made the more harrowing by constant awareness of the imminence of death. In those early years of the nineteenth century, when knowledge of asepsis was almost nil and, for all his dedication, a doctor's practice had, perforce, to *be* a "practice," the harsh New England winter took its regular toll of victims, not only among the elderly, but also of the very young. When one of Emily's dearest friends, Sophia Holland, died in 1844, she had been so grieved that her alarmed parents had sent her to visit her aunt in Boston for a change of scene. Two years later she wrote of this tragic episode to Abiah Root as though she had only just experienced it; and being constantly told that her own eternal destination was in grave doubt must have shaken her considerably.

Then, in November, 1850, Leonard Humphrey, who had been principal of Amherst Academy when she was there, and whom she had affectionately called "My Master," died of brain fever. Humphrey had been one of a group of young men who frequented the Dickinson house; he had shown Emily special kindness, willingly sharing his interest in philosophy and poetry with her, discussing the works of Carlyle and Wordsworth while his avid "pupil" listened spellbound. ". . . it is indeed hard to bear," Emily wrote to Abiah. "I don't think there will be any sunshine or any singing birds in the spring that's coming." [12]

The next winter, 1851, an epidemic of influenza took its toll. It is really not at all surprising that thoughts concerning Eternity should occur frequently in her letters, or that Eternity should have become one of her great poetic themes. It is even less surprising that human loneliness should have also assailed her, revealed in the poignant line in a letter to her brother, "Oh, I am so lonely!" [13] Least surprising of all is to find in these bereavements at least one reason for her reluctance to leave her home, twenty-three years before she had made complete her withdrawal from the world. In answer to an invitation from a school friend to come for a visit, she wrote,

I'm afraid I'm growing *selfish* in my dear home, but I do love it so, and when some pleasant friend asks me to pass a week with her, I look at my father and mother and Vinnie and all my friends, and I say no—can't leave them, what if they die when I'm gone. . . .[14]

Her feelings were analagous to those of a child who has been told by an insensitive servant that his parents would go away, and who creeps downstairs after he has been put to bed to assure himself that they are really there. Much of the child seems to have lingered long in Emily Dickinson—indeed, she admitted, "I love so to be a child." [15] And her innate, heightened sensitivity made her react to both the joys and the sorrows of her life with a child's honest directness and openheartedness.

There is no evidence that she thought of Leonard Humphrey as other than her teacher, and her affection for him was of the variety that characterized all such relationships. She said herself that she was always in love with her teachers. Deeper, perhaps, was her feeling for Benjamin Franklin Newton, who studied law in her father's office between 1847 and 1849, and with whom she continued to correspond after he left Amherst. Through Newton, she learned to love Emerson's essays and poetry, and he was the first encourager and critic of her work. Her grief was profound when he died at Worcester, of consumption, in 1850; ten months later she went so far as to write the Reverend Edward Everett Hale, who had been Newton's pastor, begging for assurance that her friend had been "willing to die," and was now safely "at home":

Mr. Newton became to me a gentle, yet grave Preceptor, teaching me what to read, what authors to admire, what was most grand and beautiful in nature, and that sublimer lesson, a faith in things unseen. . . .[16]

Newton was the friend who "taught me Immortality—but venturing too near himself—he never returned." [17] He had also told her that he "would like to live until I had become a poet. . . ." [18] Again, shortly after this bereavement, we find another indication of Emily's reluctance to leave home, even to visit Abiah Root, her oldest and dearest friend:

. . . I don't go far from home unless emergency leads me by the hand, and then I do it obstinately and draw back if I can. Should I ever leave home, which is improbable, I will with much delight accept your invitation; till then, my dear Abiah, my warmest thanks are yours, but don't expect me.[19]

To Susan Gilbert, who was in the process of becoming engaged to Austin Dickinson, and with whom Emily was enjoying the first flush of excitement over a friendship which would prove disappointing—for Sue was shallow, frivolous, and jealously possessive of Austin—she wrote,

Susie—it is a little thing to say how lone it is—anyone can do it— but to wear that loneliness next your heart, when you sleep, and when you wake, ever missing something, *this* one cannot say, and it baffles me.[20]

Twenty years later, she wrote to Thomas Wentworth Higginson, "My earliest friend told me the week before he died, 'If I live, I will go to Amherst—if I die, I certainly will." [21] There is no doubt that Newton made an indelible impression on her heart and mind.

But Emily Dickinson was to bear an even more devastating experience in terms of emotional commitment. In February, 1854, she went to Washington, accompanied by her sister, for devoted brother was absorbed in a new status as devoted [hus]band and happily expectant father, no doubt urged her to [ha]ve faith," which called forth one of Emily's delightfully [sau]cy epigrams:

"Faith" is a fine invention
When gentlemen can see—
But Microscopes are prudent
In an emergency.

To the outside world she was the same Emily, perhaps a little [m]ore withdrawn than usual. Only the poems, kept in her desk [a]way from prying and uncomprehending eyes, and the rough [dr]afts of letters almost certainly intended for Wadsworth but [p]erhaps never sent, reveal the turmoil in her heart that, as she [la]ter admitted to Higginson, nearly shattered her reason. "I am [ol]der—tonight, Master—but love is the same—so are the moon [an]d the crescent," 24 she wrote sometime in 1861. " . . . I wish [w]ith a might I cannot repress—that mine were the Queen's [p]lace," and she adds, " 'Chillon' is not funny." She begged him [to] come again to Amherst, asking plaintively, "Would it do [h]arm—yet, we both fear God." 25

How Wadsworth reacted, assuming that the letter was sent, [c]an only be conjectured, and, indeed, numerous conjectures have [b]een made—sometimes lacking any quality of mercy! Without [c]oncrete evidence, all that can be safely assumed is that he prob[a]bly replied in the manner of any good clergyman, for whom [f]eminine admiration is an occupational hazard. He might have [g]rieved for her "misplaced affection," as such would have been [c]alled at that time, but there is no reason to assume that he [w]ould have been offended by her outburst.

Emily's rough draft beginning, "Oh, did I offend it," probably [i]s more indicative of her emotional state at receiving a calm rea[s]onable reply to her avowal. Especially since she continues, "A [l]ove so big it scares her, rushing among her small heart," and [r]eminds him that she "never flinched thro' that awful parting, [but] held her life so tight that he should not see the

a month's visit with her father who was then serving in the House of Representatives. On the way back to Amherst, the two sisters stopped in Philadelphia to visit the Lyman Colemans, old family friends. The Colemans were members of Arch Street Church, where the Reverend Charles Wadsworth was pastor. The only available photograph of Wadsworth was taken during the last years of his life, and the balding, grandfatherly man, peering from behind gold-rimmed spectacles, gives little indication of the dynamic preacher whom Emily doubtless saw for the first time in the pulpit in 1854. Wadsworth was then forty years old, rapidly approaching the height of those powers which would make him one of the foremost preachers of his time; he was happily married and totally involved in his pastorate. Emily was twenty-three and writing of loneliness. There is no direct evidence that he made any personal impression upon her, and she does not even mention having heard him preach, but subsequent events reveal that her reaction must have been profound.

There is no way of knowing when she first wrote to him, though it is fairly safe to say that she took the initiative. Possibly an answer to her first appeal was the undated, unsigned letter in Wadsworth's handwriting (found in her papers after her death), in which he assures her of "all my sympathy, and my constant earnest prayers," and expresses his anxiety "to learn more definitely of your trial . . . though I have no right to intrude on your sorrow. . . ." 22

Emily possessed her full share of New England reticence, but she seemingly had no objection to pouring out her heart in letters, as well as in poetry, and the circumstances surrounding her at this moment indicate that her sense of loneliness was growing more and more acute. Humphrey and Newton were gone; most of her old school friends were married; her beloved brother was engaged to Susan Gilbert and they were preparing for their marriage in 1856. That her "affliction," as Wadsworth expressed it, might have been a deep depression due to her increasing sense of isolation is not beyond belief; that she should turn for help to a comparative stranger is quite possible. There was no one in Amherst in whom she could or would confide. That Wadsworth should have replied sympathetically is also quite consistent. A clergyman of the 1850's would have taken with utmost seriousness—indeed welcomed—such a call to his responsibility as a physician of souls. And Emily was a friend of two valued parishioners. No more reason or introduction would have been necessary.

Among Emily's papers, rough drafts of several letters were found, addressed to "Dear Master." Handwriting and internal evidence date them from 1858 through 1862, but their existence does not preclude the possibility of earlier letters which have not survived, letters which Emily might have written to Charles Wadsworth between 1854 and his visit to Amherst in 1860, which might support the thesis that, at first, her feelings towards him were simply those of Humphrey's and Newton's "pupil." Wadsworth, in her estimation, would far excel either of the two younger men in intellectual attainments, and "Master" would have seemed to her a far more suitable title for him (especially since he was a clergyman), than either "teacher" or "tutor." Certainly, it is significant that, in 1858, she began to work seriously at her poetry, and to make a definite attempt to assemble fair copies into the little packets which so astounded her sister Lavinia when she discovered them. Since overweening self confidence was not, at this time, one of Emily's salient characteristics, it is reasonable to assume that she was receiving sympathetic encouragement from someone whose judgment she trusted, and there was no one in Amherst who could have provided it. The increasing frequency of poems in her letters may also be an indication that she was trying her wings. Several lines in a "Dear Master" rough draft, dated c. 1858, though in prose, have much the same cadence as her poetry. One example is especially striking: "How strong when weak to recollect, and easy, quite, to love—" [23] when written in stanzaic form,

> How strong when weak to recollect,
> And easy, quite, to love—

is not too unlike one of her poems:

> How fleet—how indiscreet an (
> How always wrong is Love—

The tone of this particular letter also sugges been corresponding with the recipient for qui Wadsworth is the only person who could po as her literary preceptor during those years.

He came to Amherst in 1860, and Emily evi with him. That her love was a complex fabri bestowed adult affection, loneliness, and long does not make it the less real; that Wadswor man makes her situation all the more poignant marriage was a fundamental "Tenet of Belief" teenth century. The mere suggestion that ar could remotely entertain any kind of affectio man would have been considered not only in decent. Charles Wadsworth was happily marri same tenets prevailed for him, so there could of Emily's emotion being reciprocated. His be was also a formidable barrier. A cryptic poem in a Bowles, a very close friend of the Dickinson f known Emily all her life, seems to reflect her se tion and guilt over an emotion that tended to be

> Two swimmers wrestled on the spar—
> Until the morning sun—
> When One—turned, smiling to the land
> Oh God! the Other One!
>
> The stray ships—passing—
> Spied a face—
> Upon the waters borne—
> With eyes, in death—still begging raised
> And hands—beseeching—thrown!

Bowles, obviously oblivious to the real cause of thinking perhaps that she was feeling unusually b

wound. . . ." And the final plea—"Master—open your life wide and take me in forever, I will never be noisy when you want me to be still. I will be your best little girl—but that is enough—I shall not want any more—" [26] is heartrending. For, at the time this letter was apparently drafted, Wadsworth had left Philadelphia to become pastor of Calvary Church in San Francisco, and, for Emily, California was as remote as the moon. Wadsworth had "left the land," as she later told Higginson, leaving her more lonely and isolated than ever.

"The Heart wants what it wants—or else it does not care." [27] Self-discipline was not yet one of Emily's salient characteristics. Both the poems and letters of 1861–62 show her in emotional battle, trying to persuade her mind to rule over her heart, and she could no longer look to religion for comfort in her distress. She had not joined the church; in fact, she had stopped attending church services, except very occasionally. And Wadsworth, who might have been instrumental in her return, had, to her mind, deserted her. Yet she instinctively turned to God:

> Savior! I've no one else to tell—
> And so I trouble *thee.*
> I am the one forgot thee so—
> Dost thou remember me?
> Nor, for myself, I came so far—
> That were the little load—
> I brought thee the imperial Heart
> I had not strength to hold—
> The Heart I carried in my own—
> Till mine too heavy grew—
> Yet—strangest—*heavier* since it went—
> Is it too large for *you?*

Even her poetry was no source of consolation:

> Put up my lute!
> What of—my Music!
> Since the sole ear I cared to charm—
> Passive—as Granite—laps My Music—
> Sobbing—will suit—as well as psalm!

> Would but the "Memnon" of the Desert—
> Teach me the strain
> That vanquished Him—
> When He—surrendered to the Sunrise—
> Maybe—that—would awaken—them!

Occasionally her imagination ran riot, as in the poem enclosed in a letter to Samuel Bowles, beginning, "Title divine —is Mine! The Wife—without the Sign!" in which she calls herself "Empress of Calvary!" and to which she appended an urgent, appeal for secrecy: "*Here's* what I had to 'tell you'—you will tell no other? Honor—is it's own pawn—" [28] Yet, strangely enough, some of her best-loved poems date from this crucial period: "I felt a Funeral in my Brain," with its controlled cadence; " 'Hope' is the thing with feathers;" "Safe in their Alabaster Chambers;" "The Soul selects her own Society;" and, "After great pain, a formal feeling comes." Her words in a poem written in 1860, "To learn the Transport by the Pain," had proved prophetic. Like Matthew Arnold's strayed reveler, the singer had become the song she sang.

She wrote incessantly. The sheer volume of finished poems dating between 1862 and 1865 is astounding. Drawing on her deepest, innermost ponderings on the meaning of life, death, eternity and immortality, now, with the added dimension of love experienced and perforce renounced, her work covered the totality of human experience.

Because she recognized so completely that life can—indeed, must—be lived from within, what seemed to be her withdrawal from the exterior world did not dry up her creative spring. Emily Dickinson did not retire to a Tennysonian "Palace of Art." Her "smallest room" was not an uninvaded sanctuary; there were still the demands of family life that she eagerly fulfilled, and her letters reveal how much she treasured her friends, whom she called "my estate." Certainly she never permitted herself to be uninvolved, but she was one of those unique individuals who understood the paradox of leaving the world for a sojourn in the wilderness, in order to know and love the world better. Naturally this was rarely understood by others, among whom her family must to a certain extent be included, though they respected her wishes, and stood by her protectively. It *was* considered a rather eccentric state of affairs for which unrequited love was blamed, and Wadsworth certainly did play a major role in her choice.

It has been said that we are innocent or evil only as our experiences make us, and Emily learned from experience. When, several years later, she fell in love with Otis Lord, one of the associate justices of the Supreme Court of Massachusetts who had been a family friend for years, her admission and expression of her love was in terms that even a St. Teresa of Avila would have understood and approved: "I confess that I love him—I rejoice that I love him—I thank the maker of Heaven and Earth that gave me him to love." [29] That she was capable of such loving was quite as much a joy to her as love itself. It held none of the bitterness, the tumultuous agony that beset her during the Wadsworth episode; no doubt this was partly because Otis Lord reciprocated and was eager to marry her. But also, by that time, she knew herself better. "Oh, my too beloved, save me from the idolatry that would crush us both." [30] With keen insight, she recognized that she would not be satisfied with less than complete commitment and, if the recipient did not have an equal capacity for it himself, there would only be heartbreak later. There is no gainsaying that her love for Otis Lord was deep and genuine, but there was another commitment of even greater magnitude—her poetry.

Her decision to continue on her chosen path made professional advice imperative. Humphrey, Newton, and Wadsworth, all of whom had believed in her ability and encouraged her to continue, were gone. She had continued along the lines her intuitive genius had dictated, but she was fully aware of the limitations of her own judgment. So, on April 15th, 1862, she took a decisive and daring step. Having read an article in the

Atlantic Monthly, "Advice to a Young Poet," she wrote a letter to the author, Thomas Wentworth Higginson:

> Mr. Higginson,—Are you too deeply occupied to say if my verse is alive?
>
> The mind is so near itself it cannot see distinctly, and I have none to ask.
>
> Should you think it breathed, and had you the leisure to tell me, I should feel quick gratitude.
>
> If I make the mistake, that you dared to tell me would give me sincere honor towards you.
>
> I inclose my name, asking you, if you please, sir, to tell me what is true?
>
> That you will not betray me it is needless to ask, since honor is its own pawn.[31]

She did not sign it. Instead, she wrote her name on a card and enclosed it in a separate envelope, as if to emphasize her request that he tell no one who she was. But there may have been another reason. She also enclosed four poems—"Safe in their Alabaster Chambers," "The nearest Dream recedes—unrealized," "We play at Paste," and "I'll tell you how the Sun rose." Higginson was known for his interest in the work of feminine writers, and at a time when such work was not generally judged on its merits, as the assumption of masculine pseudonyms by the Brontë sisters and Mary Ann Evans clearly proves. But Emily Dickinson did not yet consider herself an Ellis Bell or a George Eliot. It evidently did not occur to her to follow the same procedure; but neither was she willing to be numbered among the "poetesses" who filled the *Annuals* and the newspaper "Poet's Corners." Perhaps she thought, mischievously, that her letter would interest Higginson sufficiently to induce him to read her poems before he looked at her name.

Higginson, one of the most prolific writers and popular Lyceum speakers of the day, whose outspoken support of various liberal causes—especially that of anti-slavery—ultimately caused his resignation from the ministry, was definitely intrigued. (The fact that, in 1862, he was still a clergyman may have had considerable weight in Emily's choice of him as a "preceptor," rather than of Emerson or Lowell, with whom she was equally unacquainted, but who lacked the clerical sanction.) "The impression of a wholly new and original poetic genius was as distinct on my mind at the reading of these four poems as it is now, after half a century of further knowledge," he wrote in an article for the *Atlantic* in 1891.

. . . and with it came the problem never yet solved, what place ought to be assigned in literature to what is so remarkable, yet so elusive of criticism. The bee did not evade the schoolboy more than she evaded me; and even at this day, I still stand somewhat bewildered, like the boy.[32]

He "ventured on some criticisms," which Emily in her reply called "surgery"—chiefly that her poetry was "spasmodic" (a technique she had perhaps unconsciously absorbed from reading her favorite Elizabeth Barrett Browning, who had been influenced by the so-called "Spasmodic School" of poetry) and that it lacked control and form. Clearly Higginson was taken aback by the uniqueness of this poetry which was so unlike any he had ever read before. And he must be forgiven for not immediately recognizing that Emily Dickinson was creating a new style, a new mode of poetic expression.

Nevertheless, he was curious. His letter to her asked for details about her life, her family, her reading, to which Emily provided answers in her usual charming, cryptic manner, evading an inquiry about her age by saying, "I made no verse—but one or two—until this winter—Sir—." [33] This was a deliberate misstatement, for she had already written upwards of three hundred poems, unless she considered those written prior to 1861 as literary exercises by which she had learned her craft. With her second letter of April 22nd, she enclosed three more poems, and added with a touch of pride,

Two Editors of Journals came to my Father's house, this winter—
they asked me for my Mind—and when I asked them "Why,"
they said I was penurious—and they would use it for the World.

I could not weigh Myself—Myself.[34]

Actually, two of her poems had already been published in the
Springfield *Republican*, but they had been substantially altered
by the editors. Like any creative artist, Emily Dickinson wanted
her work to be presented precisely as she had written it. What
she wanted Higginson to judge was whether the quality of her
poetry gave her the right to insist upon this.

Higginson was not encouraging. He admired her originality—
he was too astute a judge of literature not to recognize genius
when he saw it—but plainly he did not know what to make of
this completely new and different kind of poetry. It was not so
much a question of form, because her stanzaic patterns could
be found in any hymnbook, but her expression baffled him:

She almost always grasped whatever she sought, but with some
fracture of grammar and dictionary on the way. Often, too, she
was obscure, and sometimes inscrutable; and though obscurity is
sometimes, in Coleridge's phrase, a compliment to the reader, yet
it is never safe to press this compliment too hard.[35]

Judging from Emily's letter of June 7, he had told her that
her work was unpublishable. "I smiled when you suggest that I
delay 'to publish'—that being foreign to my thought as Firma-
ment to Fin—" she wrote, a statement of *post hoc* rationalizing,
surely, considering her initial inquiry. But the next line makes
clear her resolution to seek, above all else, integrity as an artist:
"If fame belonged to me, I could not escape her—if she did not,
the longest day would pass me on the chase—and the approba-
tion of my Dog would for-sake me—then—My Barefoot Rank
is better—." [36] The beautiful poem which follows, "As if I asked
a common Alms," gains poignancy in this context. The letter

concludes with the plea, "But, will you be my Preceptor, Mr. Higginson?"

In this letter, Emily Dickinson reveals the ambivalence of the artist who knows that his creation may not receive his own immediate world's appreciation, but who, at the same time, clings to a slender hope. Yet she could not bring herself to conform to Higginson's precepts regarding poetry, nor regularize her rhyme and meter to suit the prevailing taste. Even less could she deny those flashes of insight which words arranged in any other way than the one she chose could not convey. She continued to write to him and to sign herself "Your Scholar," and was even grateful for his friendship and the genuinely kind interest which had helped her through the bitter time when she had struggled with her impossibly bestowed love for Charles Wadsworth, "You were not aware that you had saved my life," [37] she wrote in all sincerity. Higginson sent her books, urged her to visit him in Boston, an invitation which she gently but firmly declined. He also brought the one "literary friendship" which she admitted into her life, for through him she met Helen Hunt Jackson, now remembered chiefly for her novel *Ramona*, but in the 1870's praised as one of America's best poets. She appreciated deeply all that he did for her, and valued him as her "safest friend," but gave him no say over her poetry.

She continued to live as she had always lived, in the red brick house on Main Street, nursing first her father and then her mother through their last illnesses, writing in secret, becoming more and more the Amherst legend.

Recurrent attacks of nephritis weakened her increasingly, until death came quietly—and, to use her own word, "kindly"— on a beautiful spring day, May 15th, 1886. During the brief services, Thomas Wentworth Higginson, who had come up from Boston, read aloud a poem by Emily Brontë. A few days later, her sister Lavinia discovered those carefully sewn paper packets inscribed in birdtrack-like caligraphy, containing a poet's "Letter to the World." Emily had renounced immediate fame for immortality—but it would be foolish to assume that this renunciation was effected painlessly. It is interesting to set the poem, "As if I asked a common Alms," side by side with the one beginning "I asked no other thing," and, very tempting, to identify the sneering, button-twirling "Mighty Merchant" with Mr. Thomas Wentworth Higginson. Emily was capable of both resentment and anger, and it is impossible to imagine her accepting such imperative criticism of what she *knew* to be some of her finest work in a spirit of calm resignation.

If her own time failed her, however, a later age has hardly caught up with her. Some of the greatest scholars and critics of the twentieth century have applied themselves to interpreting Emily Dickinson, and their work can be numbered in volumes. Her principal themes have been discussed, her metaphors analyzed, her diction dissected, and all enjoyed. But one of the most important aspects of any poet's work is the revelation of that poet's attitude towards poetry itself, for it is from that attitude that all the components of his art arise. To cite a very simple example, which, incidentally, indicates that Emily Dickinson possessed a considerable sense of humor, why should she have chosen to delineate her sister-in-law's temperamental outbursts in this manner?

> Volcanoes be in Sicily
> And South America
> I judge from my Geography—
> Volcanoes nearer here
> A Lava step at any time
> Am I inclined to climb—
> A crater I may contemplate
> Vesuvius at home.

It *is* cryptic, but witty, and, judging from accounts of Susan Gilbert Dickinson, singularly apt. It is also wholly expressive of the recluse Emily Dickinson who had no need to leave the confines of the house on Main Street to witness a cataclysm of nature. An exploding volcano in Sicily—an explosion in the a month's visit with her father who was then serving in the House of Representatives. On the way back to Amherst, the two sisters stopped in Philadelphia to visit the Lyman Colemans, old family friends. The Colemans were members of Arch Street Church, where the Reverend Charles Wadsworth was pastor. The only available photograph of Wadsworth was taken during the last years of his life, and the balding, grandfatherly man, peering from behind gold-rimmed spectacles, gives little indication of the dynamic preacher whom Emily doubtless saw for the first time in the pulpit in 1854. Wadsworth was then forty years old, rapidly approaching the height of those powers which would make him one of the foremost preachers of his time; he was happily married and totally involved in his pastorate. Emily was twenty-three and writing of loneliness. There is no direct evidence that he made any personal impression upon her, and she does not even mention having heard him preach, but subsequent events reveal that her reaction must have been profound.

There is no way of knowing when she first wrote to him, though it is fairly safe to say that she took the initiative. Possibly an answer to her first appeal was the undated, unsigned letter in Wadsworth's handwriting (found in her papers after her death), in which he assures her of "all my sympathy, and my constant earnest prayers," and expresses his anxiety "to learn more definitely of your trial . . . though I have no right to intrude on your sorrow. . . ." [22]

Emily possessed her full share of New England reticence, but she seemingly had no objection to pouring out her heart in letters, as well as in poetry, and the circumstances surrounding her at this moment indicate that her sense of loneliness was growing more and more acute. Humphrey and Newton were gone; most of her old school friends were married; her beloved brother was engaged to Susan Gilbert and they were preparing for their marriage in 1856. That her "affliction," as Wadsworth expressed it, might have been a deep depression due to her increasing sense of isolation is not beyond belief; that she should turn for help to a comparative stranger is quite possible. There was no one in Amherst in whom she could or would confide. That Wadsworth should have replied sympathetically is also quite consistent. A clergyman of the 1850's would have taken with utmost seriousness—indeed welcomed—such a call to his responsibility as a physician of souls. And Emily was a friend of two valued parishioners. No more reason or introduction would have been necessary.

Among Emily's papers, rough drafts of several letters were found, addressed to "Dear Master." Handwriting and internal evidence date them from 1858 through 1862, but their existence does not preclude the possibility of earlier letters which have not survived, letters which Emily might have written to Charles Wadsworth between 1854 and his visit to Amherst in 1860, which might support the thesis that, at first, her feelings towards him were simply those of Humphrey's and Newton's "pupil." Wadsworth, in her estimation, would far excel either of the two younger men in intellectual attainments, and "Master" would have seemed to her a far more suitable title for him (especially since he was a clergyman), than either "teacher" or "tutor." Certainly, it is significant that, in 1858, she began to work seriously at her poetry, and to make a definite attempt to assemble fair copies into the little packets which so astounded her sister Lavinia when she discovered them. Since overweening self confidence was not, at this time, one of Emily's salient characteristics, it is reasonable to assume that she was receiving sympathetic encouragement from someone whose judgment she trusted, and there was no one in Amherst who could have provided it. The increasing frequency of poems in her letters may also be an indication that she was trying her wings. Several lines in a "Dear Master" rough draft, dated c. 1858, though in prose, have much the same cadence as her poetry. One example is especially striking: "How strong when weak to recollect, and easy, quite, to love—" [23] when written in stanzaic form,

> How strong when weak to recollect,
> And easy, quite, to love—

is not too unlike one of her poems:

> How fleet—how indiscreet an one—
> How always wrong is Love—

The tone of this particular letter also suggests that Emily had been corresponding with the recipient for quite some time, and Wadsworth is the only person who could possibly have served as her literary preceptor during those years.

He came to Amherst in 1860, and Emily evidently fell in love with him. That her love was a complex fabric of hitherto unbestowed adult affection, loneliness, and longing for sympathy does not make it the less real; that Wadsworth was a married man makes her situation all the more poignant. The sanctity of marriage was a fundamental "Tenet of Belief" in the mid-nineteenth century. The mere suggestion that an unmarried girl could remotely entertain any kind of affection for a married man would have been considered not only indelicate, but indecent. Charles Wadsworth was happily married, too, and the same tenets prevailed for him, so there could be no possibility of Emily's emotion being reciprocated. His being a clergyman was also a formidable barrier. A cryptic poem in a note to Samuel Bowles, a very close friend of the Dickinson family who had known Emily all her life, seems to reflect her sense of desperation and guilt over an emotion that tended to be overwhelming:

> Two swimmers wrestled on the spar—
> Until the morning sun—
> When One—turned, smiling to the land—
> Oh God! the Other One!
>
> The stray ships—passing—
> Spied a face—
> Upon the waters borne—
> With eyes, in death—still begging raised—
> And hands—beseeching—thrown!

Bowles, obviously oblivious to the real cause of her distress, thinking perhaps that she was feeling unusually bereft because her devoted brother was absorbed in a new status as devoted husband and happily expectant father, no doubt urged her to "have faith," which called forth one of Emily's delightfully saucy epigrams:

> "Faith" is a fine invention
> When gentlemen can *see*—
> But *Microscopes* are prudent
> In an emergency.

To the outside world she was the same Emily, perhaps a little more withdrawn than usual. Only the poems, kept in her desk away from prying and uncomprehending eyes, and the rough drafts of letters almost certainly intended for Wadsworth but perhaps never sent, reveal the turmoil in her heart that, as she later admitted to Higginson, nearly shattered her reason. "I am older—tonight, Master—but love is the same—so are the moon and the crescent," [24] she wrote sometime in 1861. ". . . I wish with a might I cannot repress—that mine were the Queen's place," and she adds, " 'Chillon' is not funny." She begged him to come again to Amherst, asking plaintively, "Would it do harm—yet, we both fear God." [25]

How Wadsworth reacted, assuming that the letter was sent, can only be conjectured, and, indeed, numerous conjectures have been made—sometimes lacking any quality of mercy! Without concrete evidence, all that can be safely assumed is that he probably replied in the manner of any good clergyman, for whom feminine admiration is an occupational hazard. He might have grieved for her "misplaced affection," as such would have been called at that time, but there is no reason to assume that he would have been offended by her outburst.

Emily's rough draft beginning, "Oh, did I offend it," probably is more indicative of *her* emotional state at receiving a calm reasonable reply to her avowal. Especially since she continues, "A love so big it scares her, rushing among her small heart," and reminds him that she "never flinched thro' that awful parting, but held her life so tight that he should not see the wound. . . ." And the final plea—"Master—open your life wide and take me in forever, I will never be noisy when you want me to be still. I will be your best little girl—but that is enough—I shall not want any more—" [26] is heartrending. For, at the time this letter was apparently drafted, Wadsworth had left Philadelphia to become pastor of Calvary Church in San Francisco, and, for Emily, California was as remote as the moon. Wadsworth had "left the land," as she later told Higginson, leaving her more lonely and isolated than ever.

"The Heart wants what it wants—or else it does not care." [27] Self-discipline was not yet one of Emily's salient characteristics. Both the poems and letters of 1861–62 show her in emotional battle, trying to persuade her mind to rule over her heart, and she could no longer look to religion for comfort in her distress. She had not joined the church; in fact, she had stopped attending church services, except very occasionally. And Wadsworth, who might have been instrumental in her return, had, to her mind, deserted her. Yet she instinctively turned to God:

> Savior! I've no one else to tell—
> And so I trouble *thee.*
> I am the one forgot thee so—
> Dost thou remember me?
> Nor, for myself, I came so far—
> That were the little load—
> I brought thee the imperial Heart
> I had not strength to hold—
> The Heart I carried in my own—
> Till mine too heavy grew—
> Yet—strangest—*heavier* since it went—
> Is it too large for *you?*

Even her poetry was no source of consolation:

> Put up my lute!
> What of—my Music!
> Since the sole ear I cared to charm—
> Passive—as Granite—laps My Music—
> Sobbing—will suit—as well as psalm!

Would but the "Memnon" of the Desert—
Teach me the strain
That vanquished Him—
When He—surrendered to the Sunrise—
Maybe—that—would awaken—them!

Occasionally her imagination ran riot, as in the poem enclosed in a letter to Samuel Bowles, beginning, "Title divine —is Mine! The Wife—without the Sign!" in which she calls herself "Empress of Calvary!" and to which she appended an urgent, appeal for secrecy: "*Here's* what I had to 'tell you'—you will tell no other? Honor—is it's own pawn—" [28] Yet, strangely enough, some of her best-loved poems date from this crucial period: "I felt a Funeral in my Brain," with its controlled cadence; " 'Hope' is the thing with feathers;" "Safe in their Alabaster Chambers;" "The Soul selects her own Society;" and, "After great pain, a formal feeling comes." Her words in a poem written in 1860, "To learn the Transport by the Pain," had proved prophetic. Like Matthew Arnold's strayed reveler, the singer had become the song she sang.

She wrote incessantly. The sheer volume of finished poems dating between 1862 and 1865 is astounding. Drawing on her deepest, innermost ponderings on the meaning of life, death, eternity and immortality, now, with the added dimension of love experienced and perforce renounced, her work covered the totality of human experience.

Because she recognized so completely that life can—indeed, must—be lived from within, what seemed to be her withdrawal from the exterior world did not dry up her creative spring. Emily Dickinson did not retire to a Tennysonian "Palace of Art." Her "smallest room" was not an uninvaded sanctuary; there were still the demands of family life that she eagerly fulfilled, and her letters reveal how much she treasured her friends, whom she called "my estate." Certainly she never permitted herself to be uninvolved, but she was one of those unique individuals who understood the paradox of leaving the world for a sojourn in the wilderness, in order to know and love the world better. Naturally this was rarely understood by others, among whom her family must to a certain extent be included, though they respected her wishes, and stood by her protectively. It *was* considered a rather eccentric state of affairs for which unrequited love was blamed, and Wadsworth certainly did play a major role in her choice.

It has been said that we are innocent or evil only as our experiences make us, and Emily learned from experience. When, several years later, she fell in love with Otis Lord, one of the associate justices of the Supreme Court of Massachusetts who had been a family friend for years, her admission and expression of her love was in terms that even a St. Teresa of Avila would have understood and approved: "I confess that I love him—I rejoice that I love him—I thank the maker of Heaven and Earth that gave me him to love." [29] That she was capable of such loving was quite as much a joy to her as love itself. It held none of the bitterness, the tumultuous agony that beset her during the Wadsworth episode; no doubt this was partly because Otis Lord reciprocated and was eager to marry her. But also, by that time, she knew herself better. "Oh, my too beloved, save me from the idolatry that would crush us both." [30] With keen insight, she recognized that she would not be satisfied with less than complete commitment and, if the recipient did not have an equal capacity for it himself, there would only be heartbreak later. There is no gainsaying that her love for Otis Lord was deep and genuine, but there was another commitment of even greater magnitude—her poetry.

Her decision to continue on her chosen path made professional advice imperative. Humphrey, Newton, and Wadsworth, all of whom had believed in her ability and encouraged her to continue, were gone. She had continued along the lines her intuitive genius had dictated, but she was fully aware of the limitations of her own judgment. So, on April 15th, 1862, she took a decisive and daring step. Having read an article in the

Atlantic Monthly, "Advice to a Young Poet," she wrote a letter to the author, Thomas Wentworth Higginson:

Mr. Higginson,—Are you too deeply occupied to say if my verse is alive?

The mind is so near itself it cannot see distinctly, and I have none to ask.

Should you think it breathed, and had you the leisure to tell me, I should feel quick gratitude.

If I make the mistake, that you dared to tell me would give me sincere honor towards you.

I inclose my name, asking you, if you please, sir, to tell me what is true?

That you will not betray me it is needless to ask, since honor is its own pawn.[31]

She did not sign it. Instead, she wrote her name on a card and enclosed it in a separate envelope, as if to emphasize her request that he tell no one who she was. But there may have been another reason. She also enclosed four poems—"Safe in their Alabaster Chambers," "The nearest Dream recedes—unrealized," "We play at Paste," and "I'll tell you how the Sun rose." Higginson was known for his interest in the work of feminine writers, and at a time when such work was not generally judged on its merits, as the assumption of masculine pseudonyms by the Brontë sisters and Mary Ann Evans clearly proves. But Emily Dickinson did not yet consider herself an Ellis Bell or a George Eliot. It evidently did not occur to her to follow the same procedure; but neither was she willing to be numbered among the "poetesses" who filled the *Annuals* and the newspaper "Poet's Corners." Perhaps she thought, mischievously, that her letter would interest Higginson sufficiently to induce him to read her poems before he looked at her name.

Higginson, one of the most prolific writers and popular Lyceum speakers of the day, whose outspoken support of various liberal causes—especially that of anti-slavery—ultimately caused his resignation from the ministry, was definitely intrigued. (The fact that, in 1862, he was still a clergyman may have had considerable weight in Emily's choice of him as a "preceptor," rather than of Emerson or Lowell, with whom she was equally unacquainted, but who lacked the clerical sanction.) "The impression of a wholly new and original poetic genius was as distinct on my mind at the reading of these four poems as it is now, after half a century of further knowledge," he wrote in an article for the *Atlantic* in 1891.

. . . and with it came the problem never yet solved, what place ought to be assigned in literature to what is so remarkable, yet so elusive of criticism. The bee did not evade the schoolboy more than she evaded me; and even at this day, I still stand somewhat bewildered, like the boy.[32]

He "ventured on some criticisms," which Emily in her reply called "surgery"—chiefly that her poetry was "spasmodic" (a technique she had perhaps unconsciously absorbed from reading her favorite Elizabeth Barrett Browning, who had been influenced by the so-called "Spasmodic School" of poetry) and that it lacked control and form. Clearly Higginson was taken aback by the uniqueness of this poetry which was so unlike any he had ever read before. And he must be forgiven for not immediately recognizing that Emily Dickinson was creating a new style, a new mode of poetic expression.

Nevertheless, he was curious. His letter to her asked for details about her life, her family, her reading, to which Emily provided answers in her usual charming, cryptic manner, evading an inquiry about her age by saying, "I made no verse—but one or two—until this winter—Sir—." [33] This was a deliberate misstatement, for she had already written upwards of three hundred poems, unless she considered those written prior to 1861 as literary exercises by which she had learned her craft. With her second letter of April 22nd, she enclosed three more poems, and added with a touch of pride,

Two Editors of Journals came to my Father's house, this winter—
they asked me for my Mind—and when I asked them "Why,"
they said I was penurious—and they would use it for the World.

I could not weigh Myself—Myself.[34]

Actually, two of her poems had already been published in the
Springfield *Republican*, but they had been substantially altered
by the editors. Like any creative artist, Emily Dickinson wanted
her work to be presented precisely as she had written it. What
she wanted Higginson to judge was whether the quality of her
poetry gave her the right to insist upon this.

Higginson was not encouraging. He admired her originality—
he was too astute a judge of literature not to recognize genius
when he saw it—but plainly he did not know what to make of
this completely new and different kind of poetry. It was not so
much a question of form, because her stanzaic patterns could
be found in any hymnbook, but her expression baffled him:

She almost always grasped whatever she sought, but with some
fracture of grammar and dictionary on the way. Often, too, she
was obscure, and sometimes inscrutable; and though obscurity is
sometimes, in Coleridge's phrase, a compliment to the reader, yet
it is never safe to press this compliment too hard.[35]

Judging from Emily's letter of June 7, he had told her that
her work was unpublishable. "I smiled when you suggest that I
delay 'to publish'—that being foreign to my thought as Firma-
ment to Fin—" she wrote, a statement of *post hoc* rationalizing,
surely, considering her initial inquiry. But the next line makes
clear her resolution to seek, above all else, integrity as an artist:
"If fame belonged to me, I could not escape her—if she did not,
the longest day would pass me on the chase—and the approba-
tion of my Dog would for-sake me—then—My Barefoot Rank
is better—." [36] The beautiful poem which follows, "As if I asked
a common Alms," gains poignancy in this context. The letter

concludes with the plea, "But, will you be my Preceptor, Mr. Higginson?"

In this letter, Emily Dickinson reveals the ambivalence of the artist who knows that his creation may not receive his own immediate world's appreciation, but who, at the same time, clings to a slender hope. Yet she could not bring herself to conform to Higginson's precepts regarding poetry, nor regularize her rhyme and meter to suit the prevailing taste. Even less could she deny those flashes of insight which words arranged in any other way than the one she chose could not convey. She continued to write to him and to sign herself "Your Scholar," and was even grateful for his friendship and the genuinely kind interest which had helped her through the bitter time when she had struggled with her impossibly bestowed love for Charles Wadsworth, "You were not aware that you had saved my life," [37] she wrote in all sincerity. Higginson sent her books, urged her to visit him in Boston, an invitation which she gently but firmly declined. He also brought the one "literary friendship" which she admitted into her life, for through him she met Helen Hunt Jackson, now remembered chiefly for her novel *Ramona*, but in the 1870's praised as one of America's best poets. She appreciated deeply all that he did for her, and valued him as her "safest friend," but gave him no say over her poetry.

She continued to live as she had always lived, in the red brick house on Main Street, nursing first her father and then her mother through their last illnesses, writing in secret, becoming more and more the Amherst legend.

Recurrent attacks of nephritis weakened her increasingly, until death came quietly—and, to use her own word, "kindly"—on a beautiful spring day, May 15th, 1886. During the brief services, Thomas Wentworth Higginson, who had come up from Boston, read aloud a poem by Emily Brontë. A few days later, her sister Lavinia discovered those carefully sewn paper packets inscribed in birdtrack-like caligraphy, containing a poet's "Letter to the World." Emily had renounced immediate fame for immortality—but it would be foolish to assume that this renunciation was effected painlessly. It is interesting to set the poem, "As if I asked a common Alms," side by side with the one beginning "I asked no other thing," and, very tempting, to identify the sneering, button-twirling "Mighty Merchant" with Mr. Thomas Wentworth Higginson. Emily was capable of both resentment and anger, and it is impossible to imagine her accepting such imperative criticism of what she *knew* to be some of her finest work in a spirit of calm resignation.

If her own time failed her, however, a later age has hardly caught up with her. Some of the greatest scholars and critics of the twentieth century have applied themselves to interpreting Emily Dickinson, and their work can be numbered in volumes. Her principal themes have been discussed, her metaphors analyzed, her diction dissected, and all enjoyed. But one of the most important aspects of any poet's work is the revelation of that poet's attitude towards poetry itself, for it is from that attitude that all the components of his art arise. To cite a very simple example, which, incidentally, indicates that Emily Dickinson possessed a considerable sense of humor, why should she have chosen to delineate her sister-in-law's temperamental outbursts in this manner?

> Volcanoes be in Sicily
> And South America
> I judge from my Geography—
> Volcanoes nearer here
> A Lava step at any time
> Am I inclined to climb—
> A crater I may contemplate
> Vesuvius at home.

It *is* cryptic, but witty, and, judging from accounts of Susan Gilbert Dickinson, singularly apt. It is also wholly expressive of the recluse Emily Dickinson who had no need to leave the confines of the house on Main Street to witness a cataclysm of nature. An exploding volcano in Sicily—an explosion in the family next door—have the same impact, for both bespeak disorder and discomfort. In this little epigram, the poet demonstrates superbly what F. W. Bateson has excellently described as "the poet's ability to connect the unconnectable," [38] and in a manner uniquely her own. But how did she acquire this quality of vivid insight? We know very little about the workings of poetic genius, which must be inborn to begin with, but it is possible, with some poets, to infer that a particular approach to poetry is sedulously cultivated. Emily Dickinson is one of these.

She was a great admirer of Thomas Carlyle. His portrait hung in her bedroom, alongside those of Elizabeth Barrett Browning and George Eliot, and his teaching that each individual should work towards the betterment of the world, even at the cost of personal pleasure, doubtless appealed to her deeply inbred strain of New England puritanism. Certainly she must have read, perhaps even discussed with Humphrey and Newton, Carlyle's "The Hero as Poet," published in *Heroes and Hero Worship* in 1841. In this essay, Carlyle emphasized the timeless quality of the poet: "The Poet is a heroic figure belonging to all ages; whom all ages possess . . . . ," a congenial sentiment for one who hoped for immortality if she were denied present fame. A little further on, Carlyle said, "All deep things are song . . . Poetry, therefore, we will call *musical thought*. A poet is he who *thinks* in that manner." And a musical thought he defines as:

. . . one spoken by a mind that has penetrated into the innermost heart of things; detected the inner mystery of it, namely the *melody* that lies hidden within it; the inward harmony of coherence which is its soul, whereby it exists, and has a right to be, here in this world.

In other words, for Carlyle, a real poet is one who sees beneath surface chaos and penetrates to the underlying grand design in all its intended perfection. He notes that, in Latin, the word *vates* meant both poet and seer:

But now, I say, whoever may forget this divine mystery, the *Vates*, whether Prophet or Poet, has penetrated into it; is a man sent hither to make it more impressively known to us. That is always his message; he is to reveal that to us—that sacred mystery which he more than others lives ever present with.

Then, the lines which certainly must have brought Emily to the shock of recognition:

While others forget it, he knows it;—I might say, he has been driven to know it; without consent being asked of *him*, he finds himself living in it, bound to live in it. Once more, here is no hearsay, but insight and belief. . . .

And, naturally, this "sacred mystery" is beauty—true beauty. So Emily, without consent having been asked, finds herself in constant awareness of it:

> Beauty crowds me till I die
> Beauty mercy have on me
> But if I expire today
> Let it be in sight of thee.

That Carlyle's view of the poet's role and mission influenced all poets of the Victorian era, both English and American, is so well known as to require no comment. Emily, in her omniverous reading, certainly came upon Robert Browning's "Childe Roland to the Dark Tower Came," and perhaps grasped intuitively that the poet was describing the terrors of the creative quest, just as Tennyson, in "The Poet," which she must also have read, described its triumphs. Above all, from Carlyle she would have grasped his astringent premise that the poet's duty was to communicate his vision, whether or not it was understood. He must possess integrity. "He is a *Vates*, first of all, in virtue of being sincere." Carlyle's influence alone provides sufficient reason for Emily's adamant refusal to change any of her work, once she had decided that it communicated her vision, and, also, for her withdrawal from all distractions that would impede her penetrating the "sacred mystery" that she wished to experience in its fullness.

That the mystery holds terror as well as ecstasy is sensed by the reader, who knows, without realizing he knows, that he is in the presence of one who has penetrated it. "If I read a book [and] it makes my whole body so cold no fire could ever warm me, I know *that* is poetry," Emily Dickinson told Higginson when he visited her in Amherst in 1870. "If I feel physically as if the top of my head were taken off, I know *that* is poetry. These are the only ways I know it. Is there any other way?" [39] Carlyle had taught her that a poet's experience is a matter of insight and belief, and sometimes the experience is difficult, if not impossible, to capture.

> To see the Summer Sky
> Is Poetry, though never in a Book it lie—
> True Poems flee—

and the Dickinson manuscripts filled with variants and multiple choices of words indicate how she struggled to make language communicate her vision. But the impact of true poetry is unmistakable:

> To pile like Thunder to its close
> Then crumble grand away
> While everything created hid
> This—would be Poetry—
>
> Or Love—the two coeval come—
> We both and neither prove—
> Experience either and consume—
> For None see God and live—

Small wonder that often Emily found her vocation disturbing in its demands:

> Nor would I be a Poet—
> It's finer—own the Ear—
> Enamored—impotent—content—
> The license to revere,

A privilege so awful
What would the dower be,
Had I the Art to stun myself
With Bolts of Melody!

But, for better or worse, she *was* a poet. And she knew well
the demands:

This was a Poet—It is That
Distills amazing sense
From ordinary Meanings—
And Attar so immense

From the familiar species
That perished by the Door—
We wonder it was not Ourselves
Arrested it—before—

Her task was to discover and communicate the universal in
the particular, the amazing in the ordinary, the unique in the
familiar, as they came to her in those sudden flashes of insight
that she recognized as truth. Integrity must be absolute:

Myself was formed—a Carpenter—
An unpretending time
My Plane—and I, together wrought
Before a Builder came—

To measure our attainments—
Had we the Art of Boards
Sufficiently developed—He'd hire us
At Halves—

My Tools took Human—Faces—
The Bench, where we had toiled—
Against the Man—persuaded—
We—Temples build—I said—

In this poem is found the answer to Thomas Wentworth Higginson. A temple builder must be presumed one able to dis-
tinguish between beauty and trash; a real poet *knows* when he

has the "Art of Boards." It is as simple as that, and as infinitely complex. Above all, the poet must be willing to endure self sacrifice for the sake of his work:

> The Poets light but Lamps—
> Themselves—go out—

Subjectivity leading to the over-personal did not make for good poetry; one cannot "go awash" in an excess of sentimentality. Neither is cold objectivity to be prized, for this would not evoke the response which Emily recognized as concomitant with true poetry. A right balance must be struck; and it should be remembered that Emily was raised on the poetry of Wordsworth. His idea of "emotion recollected in tranquility" as the source of great poetry must have greatly appealed to her.

She would also have derived from reading Carlyle that everyone has a specific mission to fulfill. So she told Higginson, doubtless to that gentleman's startled incomprehension, "My business is Circumference." [40] To define precisely what she meant by this is not easy: in one poem she calls Circumference "Thou Bride of Awe," and in another she says:

> When Bells stop ringing—Church—begins—
> The Positive—of Bells—
> When Cogs—stop—that's Circumference—
> The ultimate—of Wheels.

Clearly "Circumference" is not to be found in the specifics of sound, motion, sight, or language, but in something above and beyond these which, at the same time, encompasses and surrounds them. One of her favorite authors, Sir Thomas Browne, used the word in this sense: "Every devil is a Hell unto himself; he . . . needs not the misery of circumference to afflict him;" and Browne also used *circumference* as a verb, meaning, "to encompass or encircle." Translated into Emily Dickinson's poetic language, "Circumference" might be defined as totality of comprehension or experience, on both natural and supernatural levels:

I saw no Way—the Heavens were stitched—
I felt the Columns close—
The Earth reversed her Hemispheres—
I touched the Universe—

And back it slid—and I alone—
A speck upon a Ball—
Went out upon Circumference—
Beyond the Dip of Bell—

In this poem of quiet despair, written about 1862 during her most difficult days, "Circumference" is quite obviously not equated with Heaven or Paradise, but with an unknown limbo beyond human existence, and therefore the more awesome because of its very lack of definition.

For "Circumference" is "Thou Bride of Awe." And what is Awe? Again, Emily Dickinson does not give a dictionary definition; she writes a poem:

No man saw awe, nor to his house
Admitted he a man
Though by his awful residence
Has human nature been.

Not deeming of his dread abode
Till laboring to flee
A grasp on comprehension laid
Detained vitality. . .

She is using the word in the sense commonly understood by the late eighteenth century poets, like Cowper, whose works were in her father's library: "Immediate and active fear; terror; dread." Or in the sense that Ruskin, whom she also admired, defined it in *Modern Painters*: ". . . contemplation of dreadfulness, ourselves being in safety,"—except that she never achieved Ruskin's sense of safety. Awe is what she feels when she reads or feels that which does not solely mean, but *is*. That flash of insight and comprehension which communicates the essence of experience. It is not totality, because no human can realize totality of experience at the moment of it, but it is a way of perceiving its deepest and most essential meaning. Emily Dickinson's sensitivity kept her in a state of constant, reiterated shocks of awareness of a vision that can be conveyed only in fragments. But the vision was always there, underlying and enveloping everything perceived, and one of the fascinations of a Dickinson poem is the discovery that she frequently attempts to communicate both awe and circumference simultaneously—and usually succeeds!

The result is poetry that holds the deepest truth, but that does not always express it with complete clarity. There is a strong suggestion that Emily Dickinson deliberately chose to speak in—occasionally baffling—ciphers:

> Tell all the Truth, but tell it slant—
> Success in Circuit lies
> Too bright for our infirm Delight
> The Truth's superb surprise.
>
> As Lightning to the Children eased
> With explanation kind
> The Truth must dazzle gradually
> Or every man be blind—

A Dickinson poem should be read in somewhat the same manner that one views an "Impressionist" painting, at a little distance, with eyes slightly closed. For her poetry is poetry of impression, rather than of concrete, factual statement. She knew that total truth does not always lie in blueprints, and that real poetry is not solely a matter of technical skill. Technique, too, must be absorbed into a vision of reality, transcending space and time.

"My business is Circumference." Nothing was too great or too small. The world of nature, the seasons, the flight of a hummingbird she viewed with the same intensity as the great imponderables of human existence. Her poetry is exploration on a variety of levels of the ultimate meaning of life itself, and, equally important, of the depths and heights of her own inner nature. And she enjoined others to embark on a similar quest:

> The Heart is the Capital of the Mind—
> The Mind is a single State—
> The Heart and Mind together make
> A single Continent—
>
> One—is the Population—
> Numerous enough—
> This ecstatic Nation
> Seek—it is Yourself.

But those who do so, must be prepared for a price:

> I took one Draught of Life—
> I'll tell you what I paid—
> Precisely an existence—
> The market price, they said.
>
> They weighed me, Dust by Dust—
> They balanced Film with Film,
> Then handed me my Being's worth—
> A single Dram of Heaven!

A "Dram of Heaven," by which she perhaps meant Carlyle's "divine mystery," or perhaps a heightened consciousness that saw all things whole—or perhaps both—this was worth existence, her entire being. The road she chose to travel was a painful one, but, for such a reward, she counted the pain little enough.

Through her poetry she recorded, as well, her own experience of God, though not in the orthodox sense of conversion. Renouncing the world, but still loving it, she wore her white gowns as a symbol of her own "election" to a special paradise:

> Of Tribulation, these are They,
> Denoted by the White—
> The Spangled Gowns, a lesser Rank
> Of Victors—designate—

All these—did conquer—
But the ones who overcame most times—
Wear nothing commoner than Snow—
No Ornament, but Palms—

Supremely confident in the rightness of the way she had chosen, she expressed at times a pride which, in another less humble about her abilities, might seem crass temerity. But Emily Dickinson knew that she was destined for greatness. Her New England honesty would not permit her to deny this simple fact and, fortunately, she never confused greatness with success. She was content to write her "Letter to the World," her poems, and to commit them to "Hands I cannot see," hoping for herself only a tender judgment, but for her work that acknowledgment rendered to genius. Both her hopes have been abundantly fulfilled.

Footnotes

Unless otherwise noted, all references are to *The Letters of Emily Dickinson*, edited by Thomas H. Johnson, Belknap Press of Harvard University Press, 1958, 3 volumes. Arabic numerals refer to individual letters.

Poems from *The Complete Poems of Emily Dickinson*, Thomas H. Johnson, editor, Little, Brown and Company, 1960. The poems are numbered according to the editor's arrangement.

[1] *Letters*, II, 381
[2] *Ibid.*, II, 342 a
[3] *Ibid.*, II, 269
[4] *Ibid.*, II, 261
[5] *Ibid.*, II, 342 b
[6] *Ibid.*, III, 785
[7] *Ibid.*, I, 10
[8] *Ibid.*, I, 22
[9] *Ibid.*, 23
[10] *Ibid.*, I, 31
[11] *Ibid.*, I, 39
[12] *Ibid.*
[13] *Ibid.*, I, 59
[14] *Ibid.*, I, 86
[15] *Ibid.*, I, 39
[16] *Ibid.*, I, 153
[17] *Ibid.*, II, 261
[18] *Ibid.*, II, 265
[19] *Ibid.*, I, 166
[20] *Ibid.*, I, 176

[21] Ibid., II, 457
[22] Ibid., II, 248 a
[23] Ibid., II, 187
[24] Ibid., II, 233
[25] Ibid.
[26] Ibid., II, 248
[27] Ibid., II, 262
[28] Ibid., II, 250
[29] Ibid., II, 559
[30] Ibid., II, 560
[31] Ibid., II, 260
[32] T. W. Higginson, "Emily Dickinson's Letters," *Atlantic Monthly*, 68:444–56 (October, 1891).

[33] Letters, II, 261
[34] Ibid.
[35] Higginson, "Emily Dickinson's Letters"
[36] Letters, II, 265
[37] Ibid., II, 330
[38] Mr. Bateson made this comment during one of his lectures at a conference on Contemporary British Literature, held at Wadham College, Oxford University, August, 1955, which the author attended.
[39] Letters, II, 342 a
[40] Ibid., II, 268

Poems

216

Safe in their Alabaster Chambers—
Untouched by Morning—
And Untouched by Noon—
Lie the meek members of Resurrection—
Rafter of Satin—and Roof of Stone!

Grand go the Years—in their Crescent—above them—
Worlds scoop their Arcs—
And Firmaments—row—
Diadems—drop—and Doges—surrender—
Soundless as dots—on a Disc of Snow

1463

A Route of Evanescence
With a revolving Wheel—
A Resonance of Emerald—
A Rush of Cochineal—
And every Blossom on the Bush
Adjusts its tumbled Head—
The mail from Tunis, probably,
An easy Morning's ride—

1540

As imperceptibly as Grief
The Summer lapsed away—
Too imperceptible at last
To seem like Perfidy—

A Quietness distilled
As Twilight long begun,
Or Nature spending with herself
Sequestered Afternoon—
The Dusk drew earlier in—
The Morning foreign shone—
A courteous, yet harrowing Grace,
As Guest, that would be gone—
And thus, without a Wing
Or service of a Keel
Our Summer made her light escape
Into the Beautiful.

49

I never lost as much but twice,
And that was in the sod.
Twice have I stood a beggar
Before the throne of God!

Angels—twice descending
Reimbursed my store—
Burglar! Banker—Father!
I am poor once more!

621

I asked no other thing—
No other—was denied—
I offered Being—for it—
The Mighty Merchant sneered—

Brazil? He twirled a Button—
Without a glance my way—
"But—Madam—is there nothing else—
That We can show—Today?"

323

As if I asked a common Alms,
And in my wondering hand
A Stranger pressed a Kingdom,
And I, bewildered, stand—
As if I asked the Orient
Had it for me a Morn—
And it should lift its purple Dikes
And shatter me with Dawn!

67

Success is counted sweetest
By those who ne'er succeed.
To comprehend a nectar
Requires sorest need.

Not one of all the purple Host
Who took the Flag today
Can tell the definition
So clear of Victory

As he defeated—dying—
On whose forbidden ear
The distant strains of triumph
Burst agonized and clear!

1732

My life closed twice before its close—
It yet remains to see
If Immortality unveil
A third event to me

So huge, so hopeless to conceive
As these that twice befell.

Parting is all we know of heaven,
And all we need of hell.

1451

Whoever disenchants
A single Human soul
By failure of irreverence
Is guilty of the whole.

As guileless as a Bird
As graphic as a star
Till the suggestion sinister
Things are not what they are—

254

"Hope" is the thing with feathers—
That perches in the soul—
And sings the tune without the words—
And never stops—at all—

And sweetest—in the Gale—is heard—
And sore must be the storm—
That could abash the little Bird
That kept so many warm—

I've heard it in the chillest land—
And on the strangest Sea—
Yet, never, in Extremity,
It asked a crumb—of Me.

1331

Wonder—is not precisely Knowing
And not precisely Knowing not—

A beautiful but bleak condition
He has not lived who has not felt—

Suspense—is his maturer Sister—
Whether Adult Delight is Pain
Or of itself a new misgiving—
This is the Gnat that mangles men—

1640

Take all away from me, but leave me Ecstasy,
And I am richer than all my Fellow Men—
Ill it becometh me to dwell so wealthily
When at my very Door are those possessing more,
In abject poverty—

1474

Estranged from Beauty—none can be—
For Beauty is Infinity—
And power to be finite ceased
Before Identity was leased.

1760

Elysium is as far as to
The very nearest Room
If in that Room a Friend await
Felicity or Doom—

What fortitude the Soul contains
That it can so endure
The accent of a coming Foot
The opening of a Door—

288

I'm Nobody! Who are you?
Are you—Nobody—Too?
Then there's a pair of us?
Don't tell! They'd advertise—you know!

How dreary—to be—Somebody!
How public—like a Frog—
To tell one's name—the livelong June—
To an admiring Bog!

1453

A Counterfeit—a Plated Person—
I would not be—
Whatever strata of Iniquity
My Nature underlie—
Truth is good Health—and Safety, and the Sky.
How meagre, what an Exile—is a Lie,
And Vocal—when we die—

1510

How happy is the little Stone
That rambles in the Road alone,
And doesn't care about Careers
And Exigencies never fears—
Whose Coat of elemental Brown
A passing Universe put on,
And independent as the Sun
Associates or glows alone,
Fulfilling absolute Decree
In casual simplicity—

1509

Mine Enemy is growing old—
I have at last Revenge—
The Palate of the Hate departs—
If any would avenge

Let him be quick—the Viand flits—
It is a faded Meat—
Anger as soon as fed is dead—
'Tis starving makes it fat—

303

The Soul selects her own Society—
Then—shuts the Door—
To her divine Majority—
Present no more—

Unmoved—she notes the Chariot—pausing—
At her low Gate—
Unmoved—an Emperor be kneeling—
Upon her Mat—

I've known her—from an ample nation—
Choose One—
Then—close the Valves of her attention—
Like Stone—

335

'Tis not that Dying hurts us so—
'Tis Living—hurts us more—
But Dying—is a different way—
A Kind behind the Door—

The Southern Custom—of the Bird—
That ere the Frosts are due—
Accepts a better Latitude—
We—are the Birds—that stay.

The Shiverers round Farmers' doors—
For whose reluctant Crumb—
We stipulate—till pitying Snows
Persuade our Feathers Home.

280

I felt a Funeral, in my Brain,
And Mourners to and fro
Kept treading—treading—till it seemed
That Sense was breaking through—

And when they all were seated,
A Service, like a Drum—
Kept beating—beating—till I thought
My Mind was going numb—

And then I heard them lift a Box
And creak across my Soul
With those same Boots of Lead, again,
Then Space—began to toll,

As all the Heavens were a Bell,
And Being, but an Ear,
And I, and Silence, some strange Race
Wrecked, solitary, here—

And then a Plank in Reason, broke,
And I dropped down, and down—
And hit a World, at every plunge,
And Finished knowing—then—

449

I died for Beauty—but was scarce
Adjusted in the Tomb
When One who died for Truth, was lain
In an adjoining Room—

He questioned softly "Why I failed"?
"For Beauty", I replied—
"And I—for Truth—Themself are One—
We Brethren, are", He said—

And so, as Kinsmen, met a Night—
We talked between the Rooms—
Until the Moss had reached our lips—
And covered up—our names—

712

Because I could not stop for Death—
He kindly stopped for me—
The Carriage held but just Ourselves—
And Immortality.

We slowly drove—He knew no haste
And I had put away
My labor and my leisure too,
For His Civility—

We passed the School, where Children strove
At Recess—in the Ring—
We passed the Fields of Gazing Grain—
We passed the Setting Sun—

Or rather—He passed Us—
The Dews grew quivering and chill—

For only Gossamer, my Gown—
My Tippet—only Tulle—

We paused before a House, that seemed
A Swelling of the Ground—
The Roof was scarcely visible—
The Cornice—in the Ground—

Since then—'tis Centuries—and yet
Feels shorter than the Day
I first surmised the Horses' Heads
Were toward Eternity—

1587

He ate and drank the precious Words—
His Spirit grew robust—
He knew no more that he was poor,
Nor that his frame was Dust—

He danced along the dingy Days
And this Bequest of Wings
Was but a Book—What Liberty
A loosened spirit brings—

1263

There is no Frigate like a Book
To take us Lands away
Nor any Coursers like a Page
Of prancing Poetry—
This Traverse may the poorest take
Without oppress of Toll—
How frugal is the Chariot
That bears the Human soul.

1389

Touch lightly Nature's sweet **Guitar**
Unless thou know'st the Tune
Or every Bird will point at thee
Because a Bard too soon—

320

We play at Paste—
Till qualified, for Pearl—
Then, drop the Paste—
And deem ourself a fool—

The Shapes—though—were similar—
And our new Hands
Learned *Gem*-Tactics—
Practicing *Sands*—

1126

Shall I take thee, the Poet said
To the propounded word?
Be stationed with the Candidates
Till I have finer tried—

The Poet searched Philology
And when about to ring
For the suspended Candidate
There came unsummoned in—

That portion of the Vision
The World applied to fill
Not unto nomination
The Cherubim reveal—

709

Publication—is the Auction
Of the Mind of Man—
Poverty—be justifying
For so foul a thing

Possibly—but We—would rather
From Our Garret go
White—unto the White Creator—
Than invest—Our Snow—

Thought belong to Him who gave it—
Then—to Him who bear
Its Corporeal illustration—Sell
The Royal Air—

In the Parcel—Be the Merchant
Of the Heavenly Grace—
But reduce no Human Spirit
To Disgrace of Price—

569

I reckon—when I count at all—
First—Poets—Then the Sun—
Then Summer—Then the Heaven of God—
And then—the List is done—

But, looking back—the First so seems
To Comprehend the Whole—
That Others look a needless Show—
So I write—Poets—All—

Their Summer—lasts a Solid Year—
They can afford a Sun

The East—would deem extravagant—
And if the Further Heaven—

Be Beautiful as they prepare
For Those who worship Them—
It is too difficult a Grace—
To justify the Dream—

1052

I never saw a Moor—
I never saw the Sea—
Yet know I how the Heather looks
And what a Billow be.

I never spoke with God
Nor visited in Heaven—
Yet certain am I of the spot
As if the Checks were given—

1351

You cannot take itself
From any Human soul—
That indestructible estate
Enable him to dwell—
Impregnable as Light
That everyone behold
But take away as difficult
As undiscovered Gold

974

The Soul's distinct connection
With immortality

Is best disclosed by Danger
Or quick Calamity—

As Lightning on a Landscape
Exhibits Sheets of Place—
Not yet suspected—but for Flash—
And Click—and Suddenness.

1639

A Letter is a joy of Earth—
It is denied the Gods—

441

This is my letter to the World
That never wrote to Me—
The simple News that Nature told—
With tender Majesty

Her Message is committed
To Hands I cannot see—
For love of Her—Sweet—countrymen—
Judge tenderly—of Me

Amy Lowell

1874-1925

. . . I started . . . with one of the greatest
handicaps that anyone could possibly have.
I belonged to the class which is not supposed
to be able to produce any creative work.[1]

*T*HIS wry comment, written about herself in 1918 when Amy
Lowell was in the heyday of her career, presents both her practicality and her femininity, as well as her complete honesty. Her
own work is still, half a century later, perhaps a little too close
in time to the present generation for definitive assessment, but
it is safe to say that, without her, "modern poetry" as it is
known today would probably never have attained the stature
and popularity that it now enjoys. Any judgment of her must
give this fact full weight. For Amy Lowell was not only a poet;
she literally made poetry, and the defense and encouragement
of poets, a personal crusade.

Both at home in America and in her travels abroad, she
tirelessly lectured and wrote critical books and essays directed
toward increasing in the reading public the greater enjoyment
and appreciation of that art. Nor did she confine her efforts
solely to the work of contemporary poets. Her monumental
biography of John Keats, despite its scholarly deficiencies and
highly personal tone—for nothing that Amy Lowell wrote could
ever be impersonal—still provides perceptive insights into the
work of the great Romantic. She had also considered writing a
biography of Matthew Arnold; and, in 1922, she wrote to Mabel
Loomis Todd, Emily Dickinson's first editor, "It is a dream of
mine sometime to write a biography of Miss Dickinson." [2]

This last ambition really arouses deeper interest, because, at
first glance, no two poets seem more disparate than the white-
gowned recluse of Amherst, and the vital, energetic mistress of
Sevenels, Brookline. That Amy Lowell should be interested in

Emily Dickinson's poetry is logical, for she was interested in all poetry, and Emily Dickinson's remarkable use of language certainly intrigued her. A desire to do a biography, however, implies that there is a tremendous empathy between biographer and subject, which derives to a great extent from admiration and a similar emotional outlook and response. On the surface, the circumstances of these two poets seem worlds apart, but, strange as it may seem to the casual observer, there are definite similarities between them which careful scrutiny quickly reveals.

The first important factor is that Amy Lowell was also a New Englander. She was born a Lowell, and if the Dickinsons were *the* family of Amherst, the Lowells even more were *the* family of Boston. In fact, it was often said with indulgent affection and amusement that they *were* Boston! Amy always considered Sevenels, the house that her father, Augustus Lowell, built at Brookline, her home, but there was also the Lowell town house at 97 Beacon Street near the Boston Athenaeum, of which her great-grandfather, John Lowell, had been one of the founders. John Lowell had been deeply interested in scientific agriculture, an interest which he eventually transmitted to his son, John Amory Lowell, whose remarkable herbarium eventually became a part of the Boston Society of Natural History. John Amory also had founded Lowell Institute, becoming its first—and sole—trustee. The leading scientists of the world came to lecture at Lowell Institute; and (lest it be thought that John Amory was not a competent judge in scientific fields apart from agriculture) let it be noted that he reconstructed the spinning jenny he had seen only briefly in England, and used it for the first time in America in the Lowell mills.

His son Augustus, Amy's father, carried on the family tradition, becoming in his turn sole trustee of Lowell Institute; he served as a member of the corporation of the Massachusetts Institute of Technology, and involved himself in what now would be called experimental horticulture. His gardens at Sevenels—so named because seven Lowells (himself, his wife, and their five children) called it home—were magnificent, and he took special pride in his roses, which he always insisted upon cutting, himself. Amy remembered that once her father had cut a thousand roses in three days' time. Like all Lowells, Augustus maintained certain "Lowellisms" of his own. Despite his deep commitment to science, he firmly deprecated Darwin, and he would never permit a volume of Shelley in his house. Shelley, in his opinion, was an atheist, who should not be encouraged.

Amy's family background, however, was not solely scientific and manufacturing. James Russell Lowell was her cousin—several degrees removed, but kin, nonetheless—and he had earned the family's unreserved admiration and approval, if not for his poetry, for his distinguished editorship of the *Atlantic Monthly*. And an even more important cultural influence in her life was her mother, born Katherine Bigelow Lawrence, who spoke seven languages, played five instruments, and sang exquisitely. Mrs. Lowell's father, Abbot Lawrence, for whom the town of Lawrence, Massachusetts, had been named (though considerably later than Lowell had been named for Amy's great-uncle, Francis Cabot Lowell), had been American minister to the Court of St. James.

It was Mrs. Lowell who encouraged Amy to write and publish her first book, a little collection of fairy tales called *Dream Drops*, which fourteen-year-old Amy sold at a benefit bazaar for the Perkins Institute for the Blind in 1887, proudly netting $56.50 for her contribution. For though the Lowells of Sevenels and Beacon Hill lacked for nothing that enormous wealth and family prestige could provide, there was bred in all of them the creed of personal *noblesse oblige*, the code of responsibility. If others, perhaps less fortunately placed, recited the rhyme that Amy always found enormously funny—

> I come from dear old Boston,
> The home of the bean and the cod;
> Where Cabots speak only to Lowells,
> And Lowells speak only to God.

the Lowells were constantly reminded that God should be given special and personal response for His goodness to them. Amy Lowell learned at an early age (as did most of her friends, for

that matter) that she must always do her part to make the
world better for the next generation. The ideals of philanthropy
and public service were an integral part of the Lowell heritage.[3]

Exclusive the Lowells certainly were; reticent, discriminating
in their friendships, and reserved with strangers—all attributes
abhorrent to twentieth century ears. It must be remembered,
however, that theirs was a more formal era; instant intimacy
was discouraged, and considered rather "gushy," to use their
word. To the end of her life, very few people, apart from family
and old friends, ever addressed Amy Lowell by her first name.
But reticence never implies lack of capacity for deep friendship
and affection; it permits both to grow deeply, appreciatively.
And, in an age when even husbands and wives frequently
avoided the use of first names except in private, the Lowell
reticence was not especially unusual. Besides, New Englanders
are proverbial for taking their time. "Newcomers" who remain
newcomers often for years are not unknown there, even to this
day; this attitude, however, does not imply any lack of kindness
or willingness to help if needed.

This, then, was Amy Lowell's heritage, which she never quite
escaped. Part of her nature was that of the practical, down-to-
earth Yankee trader, steeped in the straightforward Puritan
ethic of "waste not, want not," and "the laborer is worthy of
his hire"; a quality which made her publishers regard her with
amused alarm when she descended upon them. It is said of her
that, like her forbears, she drove a hard bargain. But also, like
them, she usually gave more than value received, and she hoped,
if not expected, that others would do the same. In her later
years, when so much of her time was spent in helping others, she
was generous, even extravagant in her assistance. But she was
also practical. She was known to refuse to use her influence if
she felt, for instance, that a particular writer's work for one
reason or another—usually moral—would not "go." D.H. Lawrence is a notable example. Writing to Richard Aldington in
1915, declining to sponsor a particular issue of a magazine called
The Egoist, she said,

The third, and to my mind the most cogent reason of the lot, is Lawrence's poem, which I think for pure, farfetched indecency beats anything I have ever seen . . . it would do us immeasurable, incalculable harm to be associated with such an outpouring . . . He loses his eye about things; sometimes I think his condition is almost pathological and that he has a sort of erotic mania.[4]

To an unnamed correspondent, who had evidently written in behalf of a sister, requesting help in publication, Miss Lowell wrote trenchantly, "Your letter is very pathetic, and, to my mind, your sister's poem is even more so." [5] Yet when Lawrence published *Women in Love* to a clamor of protest, she thought the book well written and went beyond the barricades to defend it, writing to him, "I think 'Women in Love' is one of your very finest books, and this suppression business makes me sick. Everybody knows that I am one of your chief champions in this country. . . ." [6] It must be admitted that time has borne out most of Amy Lowell's literary judgments.

But, while the practical New Englander was strong and, at times, dominant in her, there was another side to her nature, equally strong, which is evident in her poetry. She was a Lowell, but she was also a Lawrence, and her mother's influence was perhaps the greater because Amy was the youngest child.

Amy was born in 1874. Her brothers, Percival and Abbott Lawrence, were already at Harvard; her sister Elizabeth, at sixteen, was almost a young lady, and Kate, at twelve, was in school. The family promptly nicknamed Amy "the Postscript," [7] and she enjoyed all the indulgences and privileges of the much adored "baby sister." She was supposed to have been christened Rebecca Amory Lowell, after her father's best-loved aunt; but because that lady had always been called "Amory" and Mrs. Lowell did not favor the idea of a surname's being used for a girl's Christian name, she was given the name of "Amy"— which she did not like at all, and which she maintained, with some justification, was utterly unlike her.[8]

She grew up at Sevenels, and the gardens and stables were her particular domain. In later years the family said that she had been raised by Burns, the Scottish coachman, for wherever Burns was, there was Amy also to be found. At the age of two, she would be "driving" the carriage, seated on Burns's lap, his capable hands covering her tiny ones holding the reins. She loved horses and dogs; she enjoyed climbing trees and running up and down the garden paths. Sometimes stubborn and temperamental, she nevertheless had a generally sunny disposition, and she evidenced early that she possessed considerable charm. She adored her family, especially her brothers who fully reciprocated. The only cloud over her early days was her mother's precarious health. Mrs. Lowell had never fully recovered from Amy's birth, and drawn shades and a dimly lit bedroom were familiar childhood associations with Amy's thoughts of her mother.

No one knew when Amy actually learned to read. Her parents both loved books and read to her constantly, so it is possible that she learned her letters before her sixth birthday, when the English governess came to Sevenels. Certainly she was exposed early to language; she was never banished from the family dinner table or drawing room, unless it was a very formal occasion for a later hour than her schedule permitted, and the Lowells were celebrated for their conversation *en famille*. When she was five, she was taken to meet Henry Wadsworth Longfellow, who carried her around his dining room table in a scrap basket, and there were occasional encounters with Cousin James, of whom she was a little in awe.

As the children of the family grew older, her father took the town house in Boston so that they all might enjoy the more adult cultural and social advantages there. Amy met all the distinguished guests who came to lecture at Lowell Institute; on her mother's "at home" days, she was invariably dressed in a properly starched frock and brought downstairs to greet the guests. And she was expected, during the time she was in the drawing-room, to sustain her part in the conversation, at least by listening. Even at five, she was not considered too young to acquire social graces. At six she was sent, as all properly brought up little girls were sent, to Papanti's Dancing School; she was taken to the Boston Museum Theatre to see performances of Shakespeare and other suitable plays, and to concerts and exhibitions. It was at one of these exhibitions, when she was about five, that she saw a spool of cherry-colored silk thread, and persuaded her mother to buy it for her, just to have it to look at and hold in her hand—an early evidence of the fascination that color had for her, which would later permeate her poetry.

But reading was her first and greatest love. The first book she ever owned was *Rollo Learning to Read*. "The best part of Rollo was that there were so many of him," [9] she said many years later. The habit of acquiring books was begun early; a special oaken bookcase held her childhood treasures: *Little Rollo*, all the children's stories of George MacDonald, fairy tales, *Gulliver's Travels*, and Jules Verne—a nucleus which was eventually to grow into her celebrated library at Sevenels, which boasted first editions of William Blake and one of the finest collections in America of books by and about John Keats. What books she did not own herself, she discovered in the Boston Athenaeum, where she spent hour after hour in blissful oblivion of time, place, or homework.

School posed problems; she was far in advance of her classmates in reading, but surprisingly bad in composition. The admonishing correction, "Spelling, Construction, Punctuation," in her teacher's handwriting in red ink, appears constantly in her English exercise books. Yet the fascination for language is there: under the heading, "Rules for every day use," we find, "Put together the things that belong together," and a little further on, "The best writers always use words with the consciousness of their force." There is also a list, written in pencil with Amy's characteristic, creative spelling, perhaps intended as a classroom exercise in the use of adjectives: "Splendid, Brilliant, Magnificent, Beautiful, Lovely, Goorgeous, Shinning, Showey." [10] Whether they were her own choice or her teacher's, it is impossible to say, but they are strangely poignant, for some of

them describe unequivocally what Amy Lowell herself longed
to be and all that she thought she was not.

For, despite all the great emphasis on "Pretty is as pretty
does," a young lady was supposed to be delicate in appearance,
and Amy was afflicted by obesity brought about by glandular
imbalance. This, in an age when such maladies were not even
recognized, much less understood. It had begun when she was
about eight; on a dare from her brother she had eaten two
plates of rice at a birthday party. When she left, her coat would
not button, and ". . . it never buttoned again." [11] At first her
quick gain in weight did not cause any particular alarm; Twiggy
was not the *belle ideale* of the 1880's, and girls, for all their
delicacy, were supposed to look like girls. But it soon became
apparent that Amy's condition was abnormal, and no amount
of dieting helped. That she was painfully conscious of her
weight is apparent from her diary, where she describes herself as
"a great rough masculine strong thing." [12] There was a boy on
whom she had a schoolgirl crush, but she felt this unattractive-
ness made his taking the slightest notice of her out of the
question. "No! . . . nobody could love me I know. Why, if I
were somebody-els [sic.] I should hate myself." She felt at an
equal disadvantage among girls her own age, and this diffidence
made her put up barriers to friendship, despite her great longing for it. "I am very unhappy at my lack of real friends," she
wrote in her diary in January, 1889. Her feeling of isolation and
loneliness was probably unsuspected even by members of her
family, who perhaps had not quite realized that "the Postscript" was growing up.

To find beauty within herself in hope that others would find
it in her, she concentrated on becoming a beautifully light-
footed dancer and a graceful conversationalist; and, to her great
delight, when she made her debut in the autumn of 1891, she
found herself the most popular debutante of the season. Sixty
dinners were given in her honor, and at balls she never lacked
for partners. She went on sleighing parties and to football games
at Harvard. As was to be expected, she became a member of

the Sewing Circle, and, when the Vincent Club was founded in 1892 for the purpose of raising funds for Vincent Memorial Hospital, she was numbered among the charter members. A portrait painted about this time shows her as certainly plump, though the artist skillfully managed to camouflage the more ample curves by the artful draping of her ball gown. But her face, even beneath a distinctly unbecoming coiffure, holds both breeding and intelligence, and, even more intriguing, evidence of a dedication to some purpose above and beyond those pursued by the usual debutante. For, although she herself had not yet completely realized it, Amy Lowell had already found her destined star.

She had discovered poetry at the age of fifteen, when she had read for the first time Leigh Hunt's *Fancy and Imagination.* Hunt had confirmed her own intuitive belief that poetry is essentially an utterance of the imagination, and, therefore, a poem should be the "image" of the object that it treats. The effect of Hunt's book on her was profound. Furthermore, it introduced her to Keats and to other poets of whom, strangely enough, she had never heard. Immediately her own imagination was kindled. "What would I not give to be a poet," she wrote in her diary. "Well, day-dreams are day-dreams, and I shall never be a poet." Nevertheless, she started to write poetry, secretly, for there was always in the background the formidable figure of Cousin James, with whom any other Lowell poet inevitably would be compared. Her enthusiasm waxed and waned; sometimes she would scribble energetically, then months would go by when she wrote nothing, fearful that what she had written was worthless.

Then two events suddenly altered her life. Her mother died in the spring of 1895, and she had to assume the responsibility of managing both Sevenels and the house on Beacon Hill. Now very much her own mistress, for her father was not inclined to direct her, she began to establish that pattern of living which soon became part of the Amy Lowell legend. The top floor of Sevenels, the "sky parlor" as she called it, became her sanctum.

She rose late and often sat at her desk until well past midnight, reading, or taking notes for a biography of Matthew Arnold which she had decided to write, leaving all but the personal household tasks to the servants who had been trained by her mother and who knew more about them, really, than she did herself at the time.

Undeniably she grieved over the loss of her lovely, gentle mother, though Lowell reticence restrained any public display of sorrow, and she had to endure an additional heartbreak. A young man had asked her to marry him, and she had returned his affection with all the timid ardor that a girl who had never dreamed such a circumstance would be possible would feel. The details were never made public—even the man's name is unknown—but shortly before the engagement was to be announced, he evidently decided that even the Lowell name and fortune could not compensate for Amy's appearance, and he asked to be released. Her humiliation must have been profound. Proudly she held her head high and refused to speak of it, though she kept to her room for several weeks, emerging only for meals. And, with her father's permission, she decided to spend the winter in Egypt, hoping that sun, and a diet of tomatoes and asparagus prescribed by her doctors, might arrest and cure the obesity which had long been her affliction, and was now cause for tragedy. The diet was ineffective—in fact, it so disastrously undermined her health that she suffered from nervous prostration for nearly seven years.

The journey, however, was all that she had anticipated. She had traveled abroad before, always with her family; now her adult status permitted her to travel alone—that is to say, with Polly Cabot, an old school friend, as a companion; a chaperone, and a maid! Fortunately the Lowells and Cabots had arranged for them to have their own *dahabeah* (houseboat) for the Nile journey, for they had quantities of luggage, and Amy's included a camera and a bicycle. Her letters to family and friends at home enthusiastically reported their sight-seeing; she was deeply impressed by Abu Simbel and even more with Karnak:

The firmness and purity of line in these bas reliefs are beautiful. And there is a great deal of color in many parts of the temple. The principal colors are yellow, a brick red, and a sort of blue green exactly like an old turquois that has turned . . . And the temple is built of all kinds of materials, pink and blue granite, sandstone, etc., and all this with the intense blue of the African sky above it, & flooded by the more than intense African sun.[13]

Her eye for line, color, and above all for light, for which her poetry was to be especially noted, was becoming more and more perceptive.

She had planned to go on to Spain after the winter in Egypt, but the *Maine* disaster and the outbreak of the Spanish-American War brought anxious letters from America, insisting that she return as quickly as possible. Amy, however, refused to omit a visit to Rome to see the home of John Keats at the Piazza di Spagna, and a few weeks in Paris to attend the opening of the Salon. She also spent some time in London, where she stopped at Quaritch's celebrated book store and bought some first editions of William Blake just before sailing home.

In June, 1900, her father died quite suddenly, and Amy found herself entirely alone. Her brothers and sisters were all married, with homes and families of their own, and they were very free with advice to her about her future and especially about the disposition of Sevenels. But she could not bear to part with it. Sevenels was the source of her happiest memories; to give it up would be to lose not only her home, but her roots, as well. So she determined to continue living there.

She bought a car and hired a chauffeur, so that she could go into Boston for concerts and lectures, and, during the next few years, she gradually remodeled Sevenels in harmony with her own excellent taste. She loved beauty, she wanted Sevenels to be beautiful, and she had the ability and the means to make it so. Walls were knocked out to make the magnificent library lined with bookshelves from floor to ceiling; it was furnished with beautiful, comfortable sofas and chairs, fine chandeliers,

Tiffany lamps, and there were vases of fresh flowers every day from the gardens. The music room was even more lovely, if possible, with its marble mantle, a Chinoiserie mirror, and the only crystal chandelier known to have been designed by Robert Adam. She had always loved the painted panels in the dining room ceiling of her grandfather's house; she bought them and had them set over the doors of her own dining room at Sevenels.

She also assumed the responsibilities demanded of a lady of her position, and of a Lowell. She involved herself in the civic activities of Brookline, serving on numerous committees. Those concerning the libraries most interested her, and she was quickly appointed one of the State Visitors of Libraries for the area. She also joined the Women's Municipal League and was promptly elected chairman by the Committee for the Suppression of Unnecessary Noise. When a proposal was made to demolish the Boston Athenaeum and rebuild it on another site, she led the fight to keep it where it still stands. She even made speeches, a great innovation, for in 1900 ladies did not customarily make speeches in public. Indeed, until Amy took to the platform, no *Lowell* lady had *ever* spoken in public, a fact of which her horrified sisters, her cousins, her sisters-in-law and her aunts emphatically apprised her. Amy, however, took little notice. She had never been denied the privilege of expressing her opinions in the drawing room at Sevenels; why should she now deprive a wider audience of them if they were worth hearing? Especially when women were being urged to participate more fully in public affairs?

All this, however, occupied only the surface of her life. Inwardly she felt that something was wanting. Committee work, interesting and important as it was, could not completely absorb a woman of her intellect and energy; besides, the Lowells for generations had always done their civic duty and their own personal work as well. For a time she became interested in amateur theatricals, helping to organize one of the first "little theatre" groups in Boston. Later, in 1908, captivated, as was all America, by *The Merry Widow*, she engaged Lina Abarbenell, who was playing the role of Sonia in the touring company then appearing in Boston, for the first of her celebrated "musical. evenings" at Sevenels. Madame Abarbenell gave a vocal recital to entertain the guests (for which Amy paid her a premium honorarium), including some songs which the audience found a trifle risqué for a Sunday evening, even at a private party!

It was through Madame Abarbenell, however, that Amy Lowell met Carl Engel, the composer-pianist, a brilliant interpreter of Debussy, who introduced her to the work of the French symbolist poets. For poetry had once more begun to absorb her. The exact moment of this renewed commitment can be dated as October 21, 1902, when she went to see Eleonora Duse play in *La Giaconda* in Boston. Duse, the remarkable Italian actress, possessed a charismatic personality which not only electrified her audiences, but also occasionally unlocked the door to creative expression for others.[14] Amy Lowell left the theatre that night in a daze, and, upon her return to Sevenels, sat up until dawn writing a poem in homage to Duse: ". . . it loosed a bolt in my brain and I found out where my true function lay." [15] She went to every performance that Duse gave in Boston, then followed her to Philadelphia, where the actress graciously received her. Their conversation was not recorded, but Amy left her presence "almost on air." [16] Her vocation had found her. She was going to be a poet, a great one if possible, but a poet, nonetheless.

Night after night, after guests were gone and the house was quiet, and into the hours of early morning, Amy Lowell worked in the library or the sky parlor, teaching herself the craft of poetry. She had discovered that, although poetry was an utterance of the imagination, for it to "image" at all the poet must possess discipline and technique. And these, she knew, though it would take time and perseverance, could be learned. Poetry was

> . . . a glass that's taught
> By patient labour any hue to take.

But too much of laboring could dull inspiration and destroy beauty. A delicate balance must be kept; the poet must gain "the power of making words obedient," but the words must be allowed to convey the full force of their own power. Like Duse, she must learn to be an instrument, not a machine, an instrument perfected and attuned to whatever demands imagination made upon it. *"Le technique est la maison; le genie est la lumière dans la maison"*—"Technique is the house; genius is the light in the house." She could learn to build the house, but could she find a way to turn on the light? More and more, poetry became her life. She resigned from many committees and withdrew from many civic concerns. Time for that, later, when this task was done. She worked steadily for eight years before she sent four poems to the *Atlantic Monthly*. When one, "Fixed Idea," was accepted by Cousin James's magazine, she decided that she was ready to assemble her first volume. Two years later, in October, 1912, A *Dome of Many Coloured Glass* appeared in the bookstores of America.

She could have published in no more fortunate year. In 1912, after a long hiatus following the deaths of the great nineteenth century poets, the world was ready for a fresh poetic onslaught. The number of poets who burst upon the scene during that year is amazing: Robinson Jeffers, Vachel Lindsay, Edgar Lee Masters, Edna St. Vincent Millay, Ezra Pound, and Sara Teasdale, as well as Amy Lowell, published first or important individual poems or volumes. In addition, *Poetry* magazine was inaugurated in Chicago by Harriet Monroe, and *The Poetry Journal* began publication in Boston. As Oscar Williams once remarked, "Modern poetry really began in 1912. It was as crucial a year as 1798 or 1832."

Not that Amy Lowell's first volume was especially modern, at least in form. A *Dome of Many Coloured Glass*, the title taken from a line in Shelley's "Adonais," is quite traditional, with its sonnets, lyrics, and ballads. Only one poem, "Before the Altar," added at the last minute, is in free verse and shows either the influence of the French Symbolists or the later direction of her poetry. But there are indications throughout of that sharpness of perception and equally sharp "imaging" of it, which she had decided were the *sine qua non* of good poetry. For example, a description of birds:

> Of a sudden aslant the road,
>   A brightness to dazzle and stun,
> A glint of the bluest blue,
>   A flash from a sapphire sun.

Or of the New York skyline:

> A near horizon whose sharp jags
>   Cut brutally into a sky
> Of leaden heaviness. . . .

She expressed emotion with equal directness, as in the lyric entitled "Crowned":

> You came to me bearing bright roses,
>   Red like the wine of your heart;
> You twisted them into a garland
>   To set me aside in the mart.
> Red roses to crown me your lover,
>   And I walked aureoled and apart.
>
> Enslaved and encircled, I bore it,
>   Proud token of my gift to you.
> The petals waned paler, and shriveled,
>   And dropped; and the thorns started through.
> Bitter thorns to proclaim me your lover,
>   A diadem woven with rue.

If a hallmark of contemporary poetry is honesty, then it must be said that Amy Lowell's first volume possessed it. Later, when she wrote stories or dramatic monologues, she might choose to hide behind a mask, but the *I* of "Crowned," or of another poem in the same volume, "A Fairy Tale," is herself. And there are those scattered vignettes of the New England landscape which she knew and loved, which, though the form of the poems is different, recalls the "New England-ness" of Emily Dickinson.

A *Dome of Many Coloured Glass* was not successful. Few critics paid any attention to it; it was not even considered important enough to rouse controversy or even to merit a scathing review. Reading it today, it is interesting to speculate just how much the Lowell name had to do with the general critical condescension. There was a new generation of critics in 1912, as well as poets, who had consigned all previous American poets— except Walt Whitman and Emily Dickinson—to the ash heap. Amy, however, was not discouraged. If her book was not a "critic's darling," it did bring one incalculable benefit; it catapulted her into the mainstream of the poetry revolution. She sent some poems to Harriet Monroe which were accepted for publication in *Poetry*: in January, 1913, she went to Chicago to meet Miss Monroe, and thereafter became an avid reader of the magazine. She was fascinated by some of the things she found in it. Upon reading a few poems signed "H.D. Imagiste," she immediately realized that here was the kind of poetry she wanted to write, and the kind of poets she wanted to meet— immediately! She did not know that "H.D." was Hilda Doolittle of Philadelphia, and she never heard of Richard Aldington or John Gould Fletcher. She knew Ezra Pound only by name. Lack of acquaintance, however, did not deter her. She had much to learn, and clearly these poets had much to teach her. Six months after reading her first "Imagist" poem, in the summer of 1913, with maid, trunks, and a letter of introduction to Ezra Pound from Harriet Monroe, she sailed for London.

The poets who called themselves "Imagists" were influenced, as had been Amy herself, by contemporary French poets and also by poetry from China and Japan which was enjoying a great vogue in translation. This oriental strain was especially congenial to Amy; she had loved the Orient from childhood, when she had eagerly waited for her brother Percival's letters from Japan. The Imagists strove to find new ways of using the

English language to express contemporary emotions and ideas in a contemporary manner. They did not deny the validity of expression of poets in former centuries; but they held that, just as the great poets of the past had been innovators, not imitators, so must be any poets who hoped for greatness in the present. To Amy, who had already begun to break with the tradition of Cousin James—even while she acknowledged his excellence— this injunction was like heady wine. She fell upon the Imagist credo with gusto; she, too, believed that the poet must always "seek the hard, definite, personal word," [17] that clichés must be avoided, that "the form is shaped by the intention." [18] She said:

> The poet with originality and power is always seeking to give his readers the same poignant feeling which he has himself. To do this he must constantly find new and striking images, delightful and unexpected forms. Take the word "daybreak," for instance. What a remarkable picture it must once have conjured up . . . But we have said "daybreak" so often that we do not see the picture any more, it has become only another word for dawn. The poet must be constantly seeking new pictures to make the reader feel the vitality of his thought.[19]

Willingly she submitted to the criticism of Ezra Pound; "he could *make* you write," she proclaimed enthusiastically.[20] She met H.D. and Richard Aldington, and other poets who stimulated her imagination and gave her new insights and ideas. She worked hard.

> No one expects a man to make a chair without first learning how, but there is a popular impression that a poet is born, not made, and that his verses burst from an overflowing heart of themselves.[21]

she wrote severely, from early personal knowledge and experience. But there was time for her to see the Russian Ballet, where she thrilled to the remarkable dancing of Nijinsky and to the stunning color of Leon Bakst's stage designs. The climax of this epic summer was her visit to Henry James. The aging novelist invited her to tea, and walked with her in the garden; he gave her probably the best advice about herself and her work that she would ever receive. He himself had become an expatriate, cut off from America, never quite at home in England. "Don't make my mistake," he warned her solemnly.[22]

She spent the winter in America, writing, and in June, 1914, went again to England. She was in the midst of a heated dispute with Ezra Pound over her inclusion in an anthology of imagist poetry—she wanted better representation of her work than he had selected. By the time she reached London, she discovered that Pound had withdrawn from the Imagists, and had started a new poetic movement which he called "Vorticism." Amy Lowell had her own opinions about poetry which insisted that only the contemporary could be a source for poetic inspiration, and she had also deviated from the strict imagist rules. The Imagists, she felt, had become too involved with technique for technique's sake. She believed that there must be a place in poetry for emotion and spirit, ideals and ethics, which the Imagists shunned for fear of using clichés. "His [Pound's] work lacks the quality of soul, which, I am more and more fain to believe, no great work can ever be without," [23] she wrote to Harriet Monroe. She was still interested enough in the Imagists to continue to arrange for publication of an anthology of their work, including her own, but she also found there were other poets who had much to offer. Robert Frost was in London that summer, and she met D.H. Lawrence and Thomas Hardy who were both to become lifelong friends.

One association, however, had nothing to do with literature. In August, 1914, World War I was declared, and London was mobbed by American tourists, who had fled from the Continent hoping to find passage home in English ships. The Lowell in Amy immediately came to the fore. Prudently she had her car crated and put on the next ship for New York as freight, so that it would not be commandeered by the British Transport Office for war service. Her New England practicality evidently reasoned that there were plenty of available vehicles in London, without her putting herself to the expense of buying a new one simply because she happened to be an American, with no immediate recourse to authority. Then she cabled her Boston bankers to put $10,000 immediately at her disposal in the Bank of England. A public-spirited American gentleman, she told them, had set up an office at the Savoy Hotel to help stranded Americans with his own funds. The gentleman was Herbert Hoover, whose work was quickly augmented by Amy Lowell's $10,000 and by her own indomitable presence. From the middle of August until she managed to book passage in September, hatted, gloved, and impeccably tweed-suited, Amy Lowell met the trains at Victoria Station, carrying a large placard directing the stream of arrivals to committee headquarters. It was not an era of instant communication, so there were no television cameras to record the reaction of bewildered Americans confronted by the weighty Miss Lowell, her no-nonsense eyes peering at them through her pince-nez, but it must have been amused incredulity immediately mingled with profound relief.

The result of the Imagist experience was *Sword Blades and Poppy Seeds*, published in September, 1914. It had an enormous, unequivocal success. The title was symbolic: "Sword Blades" stood for fighting truths, "Poppy Seeds" for the beauty of dreams:

> All books are either dreams or swords,
> You can cut, or you can drug with words,

she proclaimed in the opening poem, a fantastic tale of a poet whose thoughts lay "as dead/Unborn and bursting in my head," who goes to a strange, old man who deals in words, to find that the payment he must make is life itself. "The money I demand is Life," the old man tells him:

> I sell my fancies, or my swords,
> To those who care far more for words,
> Ideas of which they are the sign,
> Than any other life-design.
> Who buy of me must simply pay

Their whole existence quite away;
Their strength, their manhood, and their prime,
Their hours from morning till the time
When evening comes on tiptoe feet,
And losing life, think it complete; . . .
Then die in satisfaction, knowing
That what was sown was worth the sowing.
I claim for all the goods I sell
That they will serve their purpose well,
And though you perish, they will live.

As can be seen, Amy Lowell had not forsaken rhyme and meter altogether. But if intention must govern form, then the intention in the title poem was to tell a fairy tale, with allegorical overtones, and rhyme and meter are therefore appropriate. Contemporaneity certainly has its place, in poems entitled "The Coal Picker," "The Taxi," and one ironic gem commemorating her disagreement with Ezra Pound, called "Astigmatism":

The Poet came to a garden.
Dahlias ripened against a wall,
Gillyflowers stood up bravely for all their
                                short stature,
And a trumpet vine covered an arbour
With the gold and red of its blossoms.
Red and gold like the brass notes of trumpets.
The Poet knocked off the stiff heads of the dahlias,
And his cane lopped the gillyflowers at the ground.
Then he severed the trumpet-blossoms from their
                                stems.
Red and gold they lay scattered,
Red and gold, as on a battle field;
Red and gold, prone and dying.
"They were not roses," said the Poet.

Peace be with you, Brother.
But behind you is destruction and waste places.

The "hard, definite, personal words" are here, as in "Happiness":

> Happiness, to some, elation;
> Is to others, mere stagnation.
> Days of passive somnolence,
> At its wildest, indolence.
> Hours of empty quietness,
> No delight, and no distress.

They are evident, too, in "Late September," so evocative of a New England autumn.

Probably the most interesting poems in *Sword Blades and Poppy Seeds* from the standpoint of experimentation are "The Basket" and "The Forsaken," in which she used what she termed "polyphonic prose," a form of poetry based on cadence rather than meter, written in prose form, but containing within the lines infinite variations in rhythm to correspond to the emotion conveyed. It is written for the ear, rather than for the eye, and is very effective read aloud. At least, by all available testimony, "The Forsaken" and a later war poem called "The Bombardment" were most effective when Amy Lowell gave them in her poetry readings. For she firmly believed that behind the poetry on the printed page was the oral tradition of the ancient bards which must communicate through words to reader, as well as hearer. It was not a new approach; other poets she admired, especially Keats, Matthew Arnold, and Browning, had observed it consciously or unconsciously, while using orthodox verse forms, but she was the first twentieth century American poet to state the principle in so many words.

The success of *Sword Blades and Poppy Seeds* established her not only as poet, but as personage. The "legend of Amy Lowell," to which she frequently and mischievously contributed, had begun, in its way almost as potent as the "legend of Emily Dickinson," though far less tantalizing and infinitely more concrete. Amy Lowell striding down Brattle Street smoking her cigar is still affectionately remembered by Boston area residents. She did indeed smoke cigars, very light lady's cigars especially imported from Havana, because cigarettes were too messy and the need to stop to light them so frequently interfered with her concentration. There is a story told of how her car broke down one day, and she stopped at a country garage to have it repaired. The mechanic demurred at accepting her check, and she suggested that he call her brother at Harvard for identification. The call was put through, and President Lowell answered the phone. "What's she doing now?" he inquired. "Sitting on the stone wall opposite, smoking a cigar," the mechanic answered. "That's my sister," President Lowell replied. "Take her check."

She lived at Sevenels with a companion, Ada Russell, who had been a successful actress in Eleanor Robeson's company, and had retired from the stage when Miss Robeson married August Belmont. To Mrs. Russell fell the task of conducting Amy's menage, and of doing everything possible to facilitate her friend's extremely active professional life. It was not the usual employer-employee relationship. In Ada Russell, Amy had found the close and understanding response she had long sought; Mrs. Russell was always the first to hear a new poem and was allowed—indeed, expected!—to be unsparing in her comments. For her part, Ada Russell found Amy Lowell a stimulating and fascinating friend, and the three-ring circus that she managed at home or traveling more than compensated for her loss of the theatre. Her composed, gentle nature was a perfect complement for Amy's robust, sometimes brusque forthrightness. It is probable, too, that Ada Russell taught her much about reading poetry, and played a large role in the success of the poetry readings which assumed such a prominent place during the last years of the poet's life.

With Mrs. Russell there to take charge, Amy could live exactly as she pleased, and she did so with considerable zest. Her many idiosyncrasies provided the newspapers with constant copy. Readers from Maine to California knew that Miss Lowell always made her own bed, even in hotels, because no servant could ever pull the sheets taut enough to suit her, and that she slept on sixteen pillows. She was known to rearrange the furniture in a hotel suite if the decor did not please her. All mirrors, clocks, and any objects that might reflect light were shrouded in black while she slept. She never rose before three in the afternoon, and dinner guests invited for seven-thirty grew accustomed to her never appearing in the dining room before nine. At one time she owned eight enormous, affectionate sheep dogs, which always appeared in the library after dinner during coffee; and each guest was provided with a bath towel so that the sheep dogs, thinking they were lapdogs, could do minimal damage to gowns and trousers. Conversation at a Sevenels dinner party continued unabated until midnight, when the last tram car left for Boston. Then Amy would bid her guests goodby, bolt the door, and settle down to write until dawn. By express understanding with her secretaries, papers left on the floor were to be destroyed; manuscripts left on the hall table were to be typed in time for her to revise on the following night. It was an eccentric regime, but one which suited her temperament, and the work that she accomplished was astounding. Poems, lectures, critiques, contributions to anthologies, letters to editors, publishers and friends, and the biography of Keats were all written in precisely this way.

When Amy traveled, her maid and Mrs. Russell always accompanied her. At hotels—in New York she preferred the Belmont, but would accept the St. Regis—she required six rooms— a vacant room on either side of her bedroom, a parlor, and accommodations for Mrs. Russell and the maid. Again, mirrors and other light reflecting objects were covered, and, in her later years, clocks were stopped. She did not like to be reminded of the passage of time.

On lecture tours, Mrs. Russell answered the constantly jangling telephone, received reporters and besieging callers, and generally kept Amy free of any imposition on her time and attention that would interfere with the business at hand. But it was on the annual European visits that the demands upon Mrs. Russell's tact and efficiency were greatest. Now the chauffeur and the maroon limousine were added to the entourage, and the luggage problem was nothing short of formidable. Amy customarily took several trunks, each designed especially for holding certain garments. There was one devoted solely to underclothing, which she had especially made for her in varying weights, and, also, in quantity, since this was not the era of "drip-dry." Once, when the luggage was being landed at Piraeus, the landing net broke, and this particular trunk sank to the bottom of the Aegean. Amy, gloved, hatted, and impeccably gowned and shod, was overcome with dismay. "My drawers! My drawers! What shall I do without my drawers?" she cried, to the convulsed amusement of the onlookers. Lowell ingenuity saved the day. She had the harbor dredged, and the trunk was recovered with very little damage to the contents.[24]

Fortunately such episodes were rare. With Ada Russell in command, Amy's travels ran as smoothly as her eccentricities permitted. And she traveled constantly, reading poetry, lecturing about poetry, and, above all, proclaiming that poetry is its "own excuse for being," as an integral part of human experience. She was a familiar figure in Boston, New York, Philadelphia, Chicago; she traveled south to Richmond and Charleston and north into Ontario. In St. Louis, her lecture drew a larger audience than did Count Tolstoy's on the same evening; in Philadelphia there was a near riot when she defended the "new poetry" against the traditionalists. She was one of the first poets to appear on college campuses; she broke the barriers at Harvard by being the first woman ever invited to deliver a lecture at that university. There was the occasion at the University of Michigan when the lights went out; Robert Frost was sharing the platform with her, and they entertained the audienced by swapping jokes until the fuse was replaced. She gave the Keats Centenary Address at Yale, and Princeton awarded her the title of "Prince of Women." At Bryn Mawr, she spoke to the "Reeling and Writhing Club" and read some of her poems. Beautifully gowned in velvet and lace, her basket of spectacles in varying strengths on a table beside the lecturn (her eyes always grew progressively weaker during a reading), she gave the first poem and was greeted by stunned silence. "Well," she said tartly, "if you don't like it, hiss; if you do, applaud; but for God's sake, do something!" [25] The students applauded. Two years later, she returned to Bryn Mawr, and opened the reading with the words, "If you want to hear any special poems, just yell." [26] Another "first" came on September 8, 1922, when she went on the radio and gave a twenty-minute reading, sandwiched between the baseball scores and a contralto song recital. Wherever she went, she was greeted with the kind of emotional response that only genuine charisma can arouse. Audiences might hiss or applaud, but never could they remain indifferent to her—or to poetry.

For Amy Lowell was a born crusader, dedicated to a cause. Unlike Emily Dickinson, she wrote very few poems about poetry, but she had equally firm convictions about what poetry *is,* and those she expressed unequivocally in lectures and in the prefaces to her collections. "All poetry is made up of two ingredients in varying proportions. They are: *Vision* and *Words,*" [27] she told a New York audience in 1915. In the preface to *Legends,* she wrote, "A poet . . . respects nothing and reveres everything, but what he loves he makes his own." Craftsmanship was important: "The Anglo-Saxon of our day has a tendency to think that a fine idea excuses slovenly workmanship." [28] Equally she deprecated the poet who assumed the role of the teacher. It was her "firm belief that poetry should not try to teach, but that it should exist simply because it is a created Beauty." [29] "Poetry," she wrote in her biography of Keats, "is avowedly what one makes of it."

It should mean different things to different people. It is at once absolute and "full of outlines of mysterious truth." Its absolute quality can be gauged and criticized; its "shadowy outlines" will vary with every reader.[30]

It was this conviction that lay behind her annoyance with D.H. Lawrence's poetry, which, for her taste, was too explicit, leaving nothing to the reader's imagination. She was severe, too, with poets who used their medium solely for self-expression: ". . . Edna Millay, enchanting though she is in her own line, attempts nothing beyond the personal, which is the hallmark of minor poetry." [31] In 1924, five years before her death, she stated her premise in no uncertain terms:

Art is not, as so many people believe, primarily an outlet for personal emotions. On the contrary, it is the creating of something apart from the artist which, when created, should have a separate existence and justify itself by its power of reproducing an emotion or a thought in the mind of the reader. The professional poet . . . writes, it is true, only when he has something to say, but, at the same time, with the object of making a beautiful poem, not with the object of relieving himself from any particular state of mind.[32]

Yet no one was more aware than she of the amount of personal anguish involved in the creative act:

I do not suppose that anyone not a poet can realize the agony of creating a poem. Every nerve, every muscle, seems strained to the breaking point. The poem will not be denied, to refuse to write it would be a greater torture. It tears its way out of the brain, splintering and breaking its passage, and leaves that organ in the state of a jelly-fish when the task is done. And yet to have no poem to write is the worst state of all. Truly, a poet's life is not a happy one. Broken and shattered when creating, miserable and void when not creating, urged always to a strain which cannot heal except through immense pain, peaceful only in the occasional consciousness of a tolerable achievement—certainly the poor creature must be born to his calling, for no man would take on such an existence willingly.[33]

And none of this anguish must show! The poet must eschew any easy way of wearing his heart on his sleeve, if, according to Amy Lowell standards, he dares to believe he has any claim to greatness.

In an era of tremendous experimentation in all the arts, she nevertheless clung to the conviction that poetry must communicate experience in meaningful language. She did not care for Gertrude Stein! Nor did she care for the new, critical approach, which dissected poems as though they were biology specimens, and concentrated on technique rather than on what the poet actually said:

Technique is only important for the person who likes to do puzzles . . . It is a scientific mechanism which follows on creation. No artist ever thinks of technique while he is writing a poem; that is all done with his subconscious mind. It is only when he has a critical faculty, too, that he is able afterwards to find out what he has done. No lay reader should ever be concerned with technique. He should only know that he is reading something delightful, and enjoy it in that way.[34]

A poet's technique is like the mathematician's multiplication tables; once mastered, it is his, and need not be thought of consciously at the beginning of each poem, any more than the mathematician reminds himself at the solving of each problem that twice two is four, thrice three is nine.

Quite as important as her crusade for poetry itself was Amy's concern for a reading public sufficiently erudite to appreciate it. Like the New England teachers who were her forbears, she spoke and wrote incessantly on the genuine need for this. "I believe that the great value of literature [by which she invariably meant poetry] is not in the direct ideas it teaches," she said in 1916, "but in the mellowing effect it has upon mind and character; and this mellowing is done by strengthening the aesthetic perceptions." [35] At the height of World War I, she wrote to a friend:

It is absolutely necessary to keep the beautiful going, and because most people are lost in the maelstrom which war brings, makes the poets of more value because to them is entrusted the duty of keeping poetry alive in a world which for the moment has little sympathy with it . . . Poetry is not a thing outside of man; it is absolutely inherent.[36]

Amy's own practical application of that statement was to donate thirty-four poetry libraries to army camps for the soldiers' leisure reading. She recognized, however, that the percentage of people who genuinely appreciated poetry would always be small. "Appreciation of poetry is a rather rare quality," she wrote to Professor Abbott of Columbia University. "It is one of the highest functions of the human brain. . . ."[37]

A function, however, could be taught, directed, and developed, provided that the latent spark had not been ruined by literature teachers. "Of course, one reason why it is so difficult to teach literature as an art is that so few teachers know enough of that art in question to be able to impart their knowledge or enthusiasm," she wrote tersely in 1920.

Let us cultivate a delight in literature before we undertake to force an analysis; that would seem to be the wisest plan. Let us try to persuade teachers to regard poetry and fiction from the aesthetic standpoint, and to train their own knowledge and taste to the highest point.[38]

Everything she said and wrote reiterated her firm conviction that "Poetry is one of the great fundamentals of life . . . ."[39]

Between lectures, she continued to publish her volumes of poems: Men, Women, and Ghosts (1916), which began with "Patterns," so loved and so frequently mercilessly "executed" by dramatics classes; Can Grande's Castle (1918), her most ambitious effort in polyphonic prose; Pictures of a Floating World (1919), which reflected her love of the Orient; Legends (1921); Fir Flower Tablets (1921), in which she collaborated with Florence Ayescough to introduce Chinese poets to the English speaking world; and What's O'Clock (1925), which contained two of her own favorites—"Lilacs," and "Purple Grackles." East

Wind, the last collection she prepared for publication, was issued posthumously in 1926, as was *Ballads for Sale,* in 1927. Admittedly, she is not a poet whose *Collected Works* can be read in its entirety with unmitigated delight by a generation nurtured on T. S. Eliot and his imitators; too, like any other poet, Amy Lowell did not always measure up to her own highest standards. But there are poems in each volume, apart and aside from "Patterns," "Lilacs," and "Purple Grackles," which are a delight to discover. And even the worst of Amy Lowell is interesting, for technical imperfections cannot obscure the unique thought and insight of a decidedly amazing woman.

From 1918 on, her health was a constant source of anxiety to her friends and annoyance to herself. Despite her weight, she was not really robust, though only those closest to her realized how serious her condition actually was. Four operations for hernia between 1918 and 1921, from which she never permitted herself time to recover, sapped her strength; she was susceptible to cold, and suffered increasingly from bouts of influenza. Her digestion was constantly impaired by variations in her diet necessitated by her long tours. Her eyes grew progressively weaker, and she was in constant terror of losing her voice. But her will was indomitable. Through winter blizzards and torrential spring rains, plagued by late trains and indifferently good hotels, she fulfilled as many as thirty lecture engagements in a season, returning to Sevenels exhausted and unable to rest, for the summer months had to be devoted to preparation for the next season. The sudden death of Eleonora Duse in April, 1924, was a great shock and grief; instead of entertaining Madame Duse at Sevenels during the summer as they had planned, she went to New York for the actress's funeral. The emotional strain of the journey was devastating; she came back to Sevenels really unable to work. By an heroic effort, she forced herself to finish the biography of John Keats, and had it ready for publication by February, 1925. But she was desperately ill, and she knew it. She managed to attend a dinner in her honor, hosted by all the great and near great of Boston on April 4, 1925; as a gesture of gratitude to them for this tribute, she made a short speech and recited "Lilacs."

Afterwards, friends said that they were glad that this, her last public appearance, had been such a triumph for her. Four days later, she learned that another operation would be necessary, and her projected English lecture tour had to be cancelled. Her physicians prescribed a month's rest, in hope that she would regain sufficient strength to undergo surgery with greater safety; she complied, but insisted upon getting fully dressed and going downstairs each afternoon, just as she had every day of her life. But, for the first time, Amy Lowell was showing signs of genuine panic. On the morning of May 12, feeling more than usually wretched, she complained to Mrs. Russell, "Why can't they let me alone? The operations have never been any good." [40] A little later, while her maid was arranging her hair, she noticed that her left hand was numb; glancing in the mirror, she saw the muscles of her right cheek collapse. Mrs. Russell and the maid helped her to the couch, and with her last coherent words she told them what specialist to call. Then she lapsed into a coma. An hour later she was gone.

The lilacs in the gardens were in full flower; when they were clipped, they filled the library at Sevenels, and later went with the cortege to the Lowell plot at Mt. Auburn. Even if America had had a Westminster Abbey, there was no question in any-one's mind but that Amy would wish to be with the Lowells.

News of her death was greeted with shocked dismay and a great sense of personal loss. Even those who had most bitterly disagreed with her had recognized her integrity, and the incal-culable service that she had done for literature. Nor did her service end with her death. In her will, she left her manuscripts and books, including the entire Keats collection, to Harvard University, and enough money to endow perpetually a special poetry room in the library, so that scholars might easily have access to the collection so lovingly assembled over forty years. Because of her, the modern world could no longer remain un-conscious of poetry; her personality was powerful enough to

make people take notice, if nothing else, and to inspire the more
intrepid to explore the paths she had blazed.

Her crusader's zeal, of course, is probably her chief claim to
fame. On this, there is no contradiction among contemporary
poets and critics. Her own poetry, however, evokes widely diver-
gent opinion, and she herself wittily scored both her merits and
faults in "A Critical Fable," in 1922:

> Once accustom yourself to her strange elocution,
> And milder verse seems by contrast mere dilution.
> Then again (for I've kept back a very great part),
> Despite her traducers, there's always a heart
> Hid away in her poems for the seeking; impassioned
> Beneath silver surfaces cunningly fashioned
> To baffle coarse pryings, it waits for the touch
> Of a man who takes surfaces only as such.
> Her work's not, if you will, for the glib amateur,
> But I wonder, would it be improved if it were?
> Must subtlety always be counted a flaw
> And poetry not poetry which puzzles the raw?

Read in the nineteen sixties, these lines may be greeted with a
certain derision, because, compared to the poets of the present
generation, her work is far from puzzling or even, in many in-
stances, subtle (if by subtle is meant obscure).

For her time, however, her approach was startlingly new,
fresh, unsentimental, and honest; and perhaps her critics should
follow her direction and judge by *her* intention, not theirs. Certainly "Lilacs" and "Purple Grackles" are likely to remain favorites with those who share Amy Lowell's love of the New
England countryside; "Patterns" will continue to appear in
anthologies. And while her polyphonic prose efforts are not
generally as successful as she herself would have wished, she
must be given full credit for attempting so drastic an innovation
in form. "Truth is truth, and art is art, and life is short, and I
am fool enough to hope for posterity," [41] she once wrote to her
brother. It may be that a later age should be allowed to render
the final verdict.

Footnotes

Except where otherwise noted, the source is S. Foster Damon, *Amy Lowell, A Chronicle*, Houghton Mifflin Company, 1935. (Damon)

The Cambridge Edition of *The Complete Poetical Works of Amy Lowell*, published by Houghton Mifflin, is the edition of poems used.

1 Damon, 486

2 *Ibid.*, 611

3 In her own generation, one of her brothers, Abbott Lawrence Lowell became the twenty-sixth president of Harvard University; the other, Percival, after a tour of duty in the diplomatic service, founded Lowell Observatory in Flagstaff, Arizona.

4 Damon, 307

5 *Ibid.*, 650

6 *Ibid.*, 622

7 *Ibid.*, 34

8 *Ibid.*

9 *Ibid.*, 45

10 Lowell, *English Notebooks*, ms., Lowell Collection, Houghton Library, Harvard University.

11 Damon, 51

12 This, and subsequent quotations from "Diary" taken from ms. in Lowell collection, Houghton Library.

13 Damon, 127

14 Sara Teasdale and the actress Eva Le Gallienne are two notable examples.

15 Damon, 148

16 *Ibid.*, 149

17 *Ibid.*, 198

18 *Ibid.*, 199

19 Preface, *Sword Blades and Poppy Seeds*

20 Damon, 208

21 Preface, *Sword Blades and Poppy Seeds*

22 Damon, 212

23 *Ibid.*, 240

24 Unpublished ms., "Recollections of Amy Lowell," by Barbara Higginson Wendell, Houghton Library.

25 Told to author by Louise Hodges (Mrs. James L.) Crenshaw, Bryn Mawr, 1918.

26 *Bryn Mawr College News*, Nov. 19, 1919.

27 Damon, 323

28 Preface, *Sword Blades and Poppy Seeds*

29 *Ibid.*

30 Amy Lowell, *John Keats* (Houghton Mifflin, 1926), I, 30.

31 Damon, 635

32 *Ibid.*, 302

33 Keats, I, 303

34 Damon, 630

35 *Ibid.*, 362

36 *Ibid.*, 415–6

37 *Ibid.*, 529

38 *Ibid.*, 533–4

39 *Ibid.*, 583

40 *Ibid.*, 701

41 *Ibid.*, 544

Poems

White Currants

Shall I give you white currants?
I do not know why, but I have a sudden fancy for this fruit.
At the moment, the idea of them cherishes my senses,
And they seem more desirable than flawless emeralds.
Since I am, in fact, empty-handed,
I might have chosen gems out of India,
But I chose white currants.
Is it because the raucous wind is hurtling round the house-
corners?
I see it with curled lips and stripped fangs, gaunt with a hunting
energy,
Come to snout, and nibble, and kill all the little crocus roots.
Shall we call it white currants?
You may consider it a symbol if you please.
You may find them tart, or sweet, or merely agreeable in colour,
So long as you accept them,
And me.

Lilacs

Lilacs,
False blue,
White,
Purple,
Colour of lilac,
Your great puffs of flowers

Are everywhere in this my New England.
Among your heart-shaped leaves
Orange orioles hop like music-box birds and sing
Their little weak soft songs;
In the crooks of your branches
The bright eyes of song sparrows sitting on spotted eggs
Peer restlessly through the light and shadow
Of all Springs.
Lilacs in dooryards
Holding quiet conversations with an early moon;
Lilacs watching a deserted house
Settling sideways into the grass of an old road;
Lilacs, wind-beaten, staggering under a lopside shock of bloom
Above a cellar dug into a hill.
You are everywhere.
You were everywhere.
You tapped the window when the preacher preached his sermon,
And ran along the road beside the boy going to school.
You stood by the pasture-bars to give the cows good milking,
You persuaded the housewife that her dish pan was of silver.
And her husband an image of pure gold.
You flaunted the fragrance of your blossoms
Through the wide doors of Custom Houses—
You, and sandal-wood, and tea,
Charging the noses of quill-driving clerks
When a ship was in from China.
You called to them: "Goose-quill men, goose-quill men,
May is a month for flitting."
Until they writhed on their high stools
And wrote poetry on their letter-sheets behind the
                                    propped-up ledgers.
Paradoxical New England clerks,
Writing inventories in ledgers, reading the "Song of
                                    Solomon" at night,
So many verses before bed-time,
Because it was the Bible.

The dead fed you
Amid the slant stones of graveyards.
Pale ghosts who planted you
Came in the night-time
And let their thin hair blow through your clustered stems.
You are of the green sea
And of the stone hills which reach a long distance.
You are of elm-shaded streets with little shops where they sell
                                        kites and marbles,
You are of great parks where everyone walks and no-
                            body is at home.
You cover the blind sides of greenhouses
And lean over the top to say a hurry-word through the glass
To warm your friends, the grapes, inside.

Lilacs,
False blue,
White,
Purple,
Colour of lilac,
You have forgotten your Eastern origin,
The veiled women with eyes like panthers,
The swollen, aggressive turbans of jewelled Pashas.
Now you are a very decent flower,
A reticent flower,
A curiously clear-cut, candid flower,
Standing beside clean doorways,
Friendly to a house-cat and a pair of spectacles,
Making poetry out of a bit of moonlight
And a hundred or two sharp blossoms.

Maine knows you,
Has for years and years;
New Hampshire knows you,
And Massachusetts
And Vermont.
Cape Cod starts you along the beaches to Rhode Island;

Connecticut takes you from a river to the sea.
You are brighter than apples,
Sweeter than tulips,
You are the great flood of our souls
Bursting above the leaf-shapes of our hearts,
You are the smell of all Summers,
The love of wives and children,
The recollection of the gardens of little children,
You are State Houses and Charters
And the familiar treading of the foot to and fro on
                                a road it knows.
May is lilac here in New England,
May is a thrush singing "Sun up!" on a tip-top ash-tree,
May is white clouds behind pine-trees
Puffed out and marching upon a blue sky.
May is a green as no other,
May is much sun through small leaves,
May is soft earth,
And apple-blossoms,
And windows open to a South wind.
May is full light wind of lilac
From Canada to Narragansett Bay.

Lilacs,
False blue,
White,
Purple,
Colour of lilac,
Heart-leaves of lilac all over New England,
Roots of lilac under all the soil of New England,
Lilac in me because I am New England,
Because my roots are in it,
Because my leaves are of it,
Because my flowers are for it,
Because it is my country
And I speak to it of itself

And sing of it with my own voice
Since certainly it is mine.

Obligation

Hold your apron wide
That I may pour my gifts into it,
So that scarcely shall your two arms hinder them
From falling to the ground.
I would pour them upon you
And cover you,
For greatly do I feel this need
Of giving you something,
Even these poor things.

Dearest of my Heart!

The Poet

What instinct forces man to journey on,
    Urged by a longing blind but dominant!
    Nothing he sees can hold him, nothing daunt
His never failing eagerness. The sun
Setting in splendour every night has won
    His vassalage; those towers flamboyant
    Of airy cloudland palaces now haunt
His daylight wanderings. Forever done
With simple joys and quiet happiness
    He guards the vision of the sunset sky;
Though faint with weariness he must possess
    Some fragment of the sunset's majesty;
He spurns life's human friendships to profess
    Life's loneliness of dreaming ecstasy.

Patterns

I walk down the garden paths,
And all the daffodils
Are blowing, and the bright blue squills.
I walk down the patterned garden-paths
In my stiff, brocaded gown.
With my powdered hair and jewelled fan,
I too am a rare
Pattern. As I wander down
The garden paths.

My dress is richly figured,
And the train
Makes a pink and silver stain
On the gravel, and the thrift
Of the borders.
Just a plate of current fashion
Tripping by in high-heeled, ribboned shoes.
Not a softness anywhere about me,
Only whalebone and brocade.
And I sink on a seat in the shade
Of a lime tree. For my passion
Wars against the stiff brocade.
The daffodills and squills
Flutter in the breeze
As they please.
And I weep;
For the lime-tree is in blossom
And one small flower has dropped upon my bosom.

And the plashing of the waterdrops
In the marble fountain
Comes down the garden-paths.
The dripping never stops.
Underneath my stiffened gown

Is the softness of a woman bathing in a marble basin,
A basin in the midst of hedges grown
So thick, she cannot see her lover hiding,
But she guesses he is near,
And the sliding of the water
Seems the stroking of a dear
Hand upon her.
What is Summer in a fine brocaded gown!
I should like to see it lying in a heap upon the ground.
All the pink and silver crumpled up on the ground.

I would be the pink and silver as I ran along the paths,
And he would stumble after,
Bewildered by my laughter.
I should see the sun flashing from his sword-hilt and buckles
                              on his shoes.
I would choose
To lead him in a maze along the patterned paths,
A bright and laughing maze for my heavy-booted lover.
Till he caught me in the shade,
And the buttons of his waistcoat bruised my body as he clasped
                              me,
Aching, melting, unafraid.
With the shadows of the leaves and the sundrops,
And the plopping of the waterdrops,
All about us in the open afternoon—
I am very like to swoon
From the weight of this brocade,
For the sun sifts through the shade.

Underneath the fallen blossom
In my bosom,
Is a letter I have hid.
It was brought to me this morning by a rider from the Duke.
"Madam, we regret to inform you that Lord Hartwell
Died in action Thursday se'nnight."
As I read it in the white, morning sunlight,

The letters squirmed like snakes.
"Any answer, Madam," said my footman.
"No," I told him.
"See that the messenger takes some refreshment.
No, no answer."
And I walked into the garden,
Up and down the patterned paths,
In my stiff, correct brocade.
The blue and yellow flowers stood up proudly in the sun,
Each one.
I stood upright, too,
Held rigid to the pattern
By the stiffness of my gown.
Up and down I walked.
Up and down.

In a month he would have been my husband.
In a month, here, underneath this lime,
We would have broken the pattern;
He for me, and I for him,
He as Colonel, I as Lady,
On this shady seat.
He had a whim
That sunlight carried blessing.
And I answered, "It shall be as you have said."
Now he is dead.

In Summer and in Winter I shall walk
Up and down
The patterned garden-paths
In my stiff, brocaded gown.
The squills and daffodils
Will give place to pillared roses, and to asters, and to snow.
I shall go
Up and down,
In my gown,
Gorgeously arrayed,

Boned and stayed.
And the softness of my body will be guarded from embrace
By each button, hook, and lace.
For the man who should loose me is dead,
Fighting with the Duke in Flanders
In a pattern called a war.
Christ! What are patterns for?

The Allies

August 14th, 1914

Into the brazen, burnished sky, the cry hurls itself. The
zigzagging cry of hoarse throats, it floats against the hard winds,
and binds the head of the serpent to its tail, the long snail-slow
serpent of marching men. Men weighed down with rifles and
knapsacks, and parching with war. The cry jars and splits against
the brazen, burnished sky.

This is the war of wars, and the cause? Has this writhing
worm of men a cause?

Crackling against the polished sky is an eagle with a sword.
The eagle is red and its head is flame.

In the shoulder of the worm is a teacher.

His tongue laps the war-sucked air in drought, but he yells
defiance at the red-eyed eagle, and in his ears are the bells of
new philosophies, and their tinkling drowns the sputter of the
burning sword. He shrieks, "God damn you! When you are
broken, the word will strike out new shoots."

His boots are tight, the sun is hot, and he may be shot, but
he is in the shoulder of the worm.

A dust speck in the worm's belly is a poet.

He laughs at the flaring eagle and makes a long nose with
his fingers. He will fight for smooth, white sheets of paper, and
uncurdled ink. The sputtering sword cannot make him blink,

and his thoughts are wet and rippling. They cool his heart.

He will tear the eagle out of the sky and give the earth tranquility, and loveliness printed on white paper.

The eye of the serpent is an owner of mills.

He looks at the glaring sword which has snapped his machinery and struck away his men.

But it will all come again, when the sword is broken to a million dying stars, and there are no more wars.

Bankers, butchers, shop-keepers, painters, farmers—men sway and sweat. They will fight for the earth, for the increase of the slow, sure roots of peace, for the release of hidden forces. They jibe at the eagle and his scorching sword.

One! Two!—One! Two!—clump the heavy boots. The cry hurtles against the sky.

Each man pulls his belt a little tighter, and shifts his gun to make it lighter. Each man thinks of a woman, and slaps out a curse at the eagle. The sword jumps in the hot sky, and the worm crawls on to the battle, stubbornly.

This is the war of wars, from eye to tail the serpent has one cause:

PEACE!

Misericordia

He earned his bread by making wooden soldiers,
With beautiful golden instruments,
Riding dapple-grey horses,
But when he heard the fanfare of trumpets
And the long rattle of drums
As the army marched out of the city,
He took all his soldiers
And burned them in the grate;
And that night he fashioned a ballet-dancer

Out of tinted tissue paper,
And the next day he started to carve a Pietà
On the steel hilt
Of a cavalry sword.

Purple Grackles

The grackles have come.
The smoothness of the morning is puckered with their incessant
                                        chatter.
A sociable lot, these purple grackles.
Thousands of them strung across a long run of wind,
Thousands of them beating the air-ways with quick wing-jerks,
Spinning down the currents of the South.
Every year they come.
My garden is a place of solace and recreation evidently,
For they always pass a day with me.
With high good nature they tell me what I do not want to hear.
The grackles have come.

I am persuaded that grackles are birds;
But when they are settled in the trees,
I am inclined to declare them fruits
And the trees turned hybrid blackberry vines.
Blackness shining and bulging under leaves,
Does not that mean blackberries, I ask you?
Nonsense! the grackles have come.

Nonchalant highwaymen, pickpockets, second-story burglars,
Stealing away my little hope of Summer.
There is no stealthy robbing in this.
Who ever heard such a gabble of thieves' talk!
It seems they delight in unmasking my poor pretence.
Yes, now I see that the hydrangea blooms are rusty;
That the hearts of the golden glow are ripening to lustreless
                                        seeds;

That the garden is dahlia-coloured,
Flaming with its last over-hot hues;
That the sun is pale as a lemon too small to fill the picking-
　　　　　　　　　　　　ring.
I did not see this yesterday,
But today the grackles have come.

They drop out of the trees
And strut in companies over the lawn,
Tired of flying, no doubt;
A grand parade to limber legs and give the wings a rest.
I should build a great fish-pond for them,
Since it is evident that a bird-bath, meant to accommodate two
　　　　　　　　　　　　goldfinches at most,
Is slight hospitality for these hordes.
Scarcely one can get in,
Than all peck and scrabble so,
Crowding, pushing, chasing one another up the bank with
　　　　　　　　　　　　spread wings.
"Are we ducks, you, owner of such inadequate comforts,
That you offer us lily-tanks where one must swim or drown,
Not stand and splash like a gentleman?"
I feel the reproach keenly, seeing them perch on the edges of
　　　　　　　　　　　　the tanks, trying the depth
　　　　　　　　　　　　with a chary foot,
And hardly able to get their wings under water in the bird-bath.

But there are resources I had not considered,
If I am bravely ruled out of count.
What is that thudding against the eaves just beyond my
　　　　　　　　　　　　window?
What is that spray of water blowing past my face?
Two—three—grackles bathing in the gutter,
The gutter providentially choked with leaves.
I pray they think I put the leaves on purpose;
I would be supposed thoughtful and welcoming
To all guests, even thieves.

But considering that they are going South and I am not,
I wish they would bathe more quietly,
It is unmannerly to flaunt one's good fortune.

They rate me of no consequence,
But they might reflect that it is my gutter.
I know their opinion of me,
Because one is drying himself on the window-sill
Not two feet from my hand.
His purple neck is sleek with water,
And the fellow preens his feathers for all the world as if I were
                          a fountain statue.
If it were not for the window,
I am convinced he would light on my head.
Tyrian-feathered freebooter,
Appropriating my delightful gutter with so extravagant an ease,
You are as cool a pirate as ever scuttled a ship,
And are you not scuttling my Summer with every peck of your
                          sharp bill?

But there is a cloud over the beech-tree,
A quenching cloud for lemon-livered suns.
The grackles are all swinging in the tree-tops,
And the wind is coming up, mind you.
That boom and reach is no Summer gale,
I know that wind,
It blows the Equinox over seeds and scatters them,
It rips petals from petals, and tears off half-turned leaves.
There is rain on the back of that wind.
Now I would keep the grackles,
I would plead with them not to leave me.
I grant their coming, but I would not have them go.
It is a milestone, this passing of grackles.
A day of them, and it is a year gone by.
There is magic in this and terror,
But I only stare stupidly out of the window.
The grackles have come.

Come! Yes, they surely came.
But they have gone.
A moment ago the oak was full of them,
They are not there now.
Not a speck of a black wing,
Not an eye-peep of a purple head.
The grackles have gone,
And I watch an Autumn storm
Stripping the garden,
Shouting black rain challenges
To an old, limp Summer
Laid down to die in the flower-beds.

Sara Teasdale

1884-1933

A lyric poet is always contemporary. He works in the changeless feelings of men, and not in their changing thoughts that shift relentlessly from decade to decade.[1]

*S*O Sara Teasdale described Christina Rossetti, in the biography of that poet which she was writing at the time of her death. In this perceptive observation she not only provided the key to Christina Rossetti's continuing popularity; she also unconsciously provided the key to her own. For, like her English predecessor, Sara Teasdale possessed both intuition and insight, in addition to imagination and an exquisite lyric gift. She indeed worked "in the changeless feelings of men," more particularly of women, and her theme was love, in all its facets of beauty, comfort, and tragedy. Her poetry is personal, drawn from her own deepest emotional experience, and it evokes an almost immediate empathetic response. "I try to say what moves me," she said once in an interview. "I never care to surprise my reader." [2] Thus, as might be expected from this statement, simplicity is the hallmark of her poetry, but—*caveat lector!*—"simplicity, the greatest of all arts," [3] is *not* the same thing as simple-mindedness. The sophisticated reader quickly discovers that Teasdale simplicity can be highly deceptive.

In an age when love has almost been reduced to charts and diagrams and surveys, that Sara Teasdale continues to draw a loyal audience might, at first glance, seem surprising. That she does is evidenced by the fact that her *Collected Poems* has gone through twenty-three printings since its first publication in 1937, and a new edition, with an introduction by the distinguished American poet Marya Zaturenska, was published in 1966. Despite the fact that she was surrounded by the ferment of the "new poetry" during her lifetime, she made no effort to incorporate any of its tenets or techniques into her own work. She went serenely on her own path, marching to the music of a different drum, and even the formidable Amy Lowell had to agree that she was right to do so. In fact, Miss Lowell greatly admired her; and, if she poked a little fun at her in "A Critical Fable":

> She's that very rare compost, the dainty erotic;
> Such a mixture can't fail to produce a hypnotic
> Effect on the reader, whose keenest sensation
> Will consist in a perfect identification
> Of himself with the poet, and her sorrows and joys
> Become his, while he swings to the delicate poise
> Of a primitive passion so richly refined
> It could not bring a blush to the most squeamish mind.

she also paid tribute:

> . . . she's also a lady who realizes
> That a hidden surprise is the best of surprises.
> She seems a white statue awaiting unveiling,
> But raised on a platform behind a stout railing,
> Whence she lures and retires, provoking a nearer
> Contact which is promised to be even dearer
> If we find we have courage enough not to fear her.

For while Sara Teasdale did not consciously try to surprise her readers, her knowledge of language, and her skill in using it for the utmost connotative effect, could evoke the fullest overtones of emotion all the more effectively because it was not deliberately set down in so many words.

Such artistry, concealed by simplicity, was one source of her enormous popularity—a popularity which, in a sense, was of great disservice to the fullest understanding and appreciation of her work. She reached the height of her powers in 1933, in *Strange Victory*, at a time when for a poet to be popular automatically implied that his work was unworthy of really serious critical consideration. During the Thirties and early Forties, on university campuses and at writers' conferences, would-be poets loudly and loftily proclaimed that the very fact that their poetry was *not* published was proof positive of its excellence! The new breed had absorbed just enough of "The Waste Land" to be thoroughly ignorant of T. S. Eliot's real intention in that poem; and esoteric symbolism, minus Eliot's great knowledge and his own genuine gift for communicating it, was the order of the day. The preferences of what Virginia Woolf called "the common reader" were considered inconsequential; the individual who wanted to read poetry simply because he loved poetry was anathema. Poems had come to be viewed as specimens to be dissected in classrooms and learned journals; poets were psycho-analyzed *in absentia*. A poet like Sara Teasdale who wrote beautifully what she felt, and meant what she said—no more, no less—was dismissed out of hand. Also, her poetry was too "pure," for want of a better word, for current standards of realism. She wrote of love without ignorance, but with a quality of beauty that cynical minds regarded as sentimental naiveté. Yet she continued to be, and still continues to be, read. Perhaps she is the example of the acknowledged truth that a real poet will, somehow, always find a heart to move and an ear to listen.

Admittedly it is easy to be sentimental about Sara Teasdale, for her life, on the surface at least, reads like a novel—a fact which seems to have excessively annoyed the post-"Waste Land" generation. To take the sentimental approach, however, is to falsify her completely, for sentimentality was definitely not a part of her makeup. She was a "Romantic" in the Words-worthian sense of prizing the immediacy of ordinary experience, and of finding in that experience—usually her own—the inspiration for her poetry. But she prized equally the quality of objectivity,[4] and that objectivity permitted her to remain detached from personal involvement at the moment of writing. Perhaps this salient attribute was due to her family background which, like that of Emily Dickinson and Amy Lowell, was solidly New England. One of her maternal ancestors, Major Simon Willard, had been among the founders of Concord, Massachusetts; her maternal grandfather, George Washington Willard, had attended Amherst College.[5] The latter had come west in the 1840's, and had established himself in St. Louis as a riverboat entre-

preneur, acquiring considerable wealth in the process. [6] The
Teasdales, too, were originally New Englanders, though patriotic
Virginians might attribute the poet's inherently romantic nature
to the fact that her father, John Warren Teasdale, was born in
Fredericksburg, while his father (the poet's grandfather) was
serving as minister of the Baptist Church there. [7] In 1854, the
Reverend Teasdale brought his family to St. Louis, answering
the call to be the minister at the Third Baptist Church, of
which George Washington Willard had been one of the founders.

The Reverend Teasdale's tragic death a year later in a rail-
way accident forced his eldest son, John Warren, to abandon
his ambition to enter law. Fortunately he discovered that he
had an unsuspected flair for business, and, within ten years, had
established his own firm, dealing in special food delicacies. [8] By
this time he had married Mary Elizabeth Willard. Captious
critics might infer that John Warren Teasdale had not been
blind to the fact that his bride was the daughter of one of the
wealthiest men in St. Louis, and certainly his being George
Washington Willard's son-in-law gave him firm entree into the
business world. On the other hand, sons-in-law of the 1860's
were expected to have substantial recommendation before pro-
spective fathers-in-law would sanction a marriage; and that John
Warren Teasdale, despite his obligations to his mother and
brothers and sisters, could convince so practical a man as
George Washington Willard that his Mary Elizabeth would
be suitably cared for, is fair proof of his own ambition and
stability.

Like Amy Lowell and Emily Dickinson, then, Sara Teasdale
was born into very comfortable circumstances indeed. She was
the youngest child. Her two brothers, George and John Warren
(called Warren) were nineteen and fourteen when she arrived
on August 8, 1884, and her sister Mary was seventeen. That she
should have been spoiled and petted was inevitable; that she
did not become an obnoxiously spoiled child may be attributed
both to her own genuinely sweet disposition and her parents'

great common sense. True, her mother could never interest her in household tasks; to the end of her life, Sara was not fond of domesticity.[9] But, in all fairness, with several servants constantly on hand, there was little that a girl growing up in such an environment in the late Eighties and Nineties really had to do. This period, called by Mark Twain "The Gilded Age," was an era of affluence in an expanding society, and young ladies who, twenty years earlier, might have willingly and competently wielded brooms and dusters and baked bread, now were encouraged to devote themselves to the pursuit of "accomplishments," which would bring an atmosphere of culture and refinement into their homes.

St. Louis certainly was an acknowledged cultural center; already it boasted a university, an art museum, theatres where New York touring companies regularly played, and a Grand Opera season in which, after the turn of the century, Enrico Caruso and Geraldine Farrar did not disdain to appear. But there was still much of the frontier left, which gave the city tremendous vitality, but which was not completely consonant with the ideals of a truly cultivated society. The ladies of St. Louis knew this well; they were constantly concerned with elevating standards, and they imbued their daughters with the same concern.

John Warren and Mary Elizabeth Teasdale were devoutly religious, but this did not preclude their wanting to raise their children in beautiful surroundings. Ostentatious display for its own sake was, of course, frowned upon; but if one had money, and gave a substantial portion of it to the Lord's work, it was considered sensible, rather than sinful, to "live well," which came to mean even luxuriously. In St. Louis, and at the Teasdale summer home on Lake Charlevoix, Sara led the sheltered, protected life that a girl of her class and kind was expected to lead during that era—it was a happy world. A photograph taken of her when she was about six, seated on a marble garden bench, holding a wide-brimmed hat in one hand and a doll in the other, her titian hair falling in ringlets over a wide lace collar, attracts a second, longer look, because of the startlingly beautiful eyes, gazing out on the world in absolute serenity and trust. She has a cherished look which she never lost; and the openhearted confidence which made her trust the entire world as she trusted her family is there, too, with all its potentiality for later heartbreak, but with its equal capacity for joy.

Early she evidenced that sensitivity which would be one of her greatest graces as a poet, a sensitivity which made her respond totally to everything about her, often to the point of nervous and emotional exhaustion.[10] Because of her highly strung temperament, she was allowed to do pretty much as she pleased, but it is generally agreed that she repaid this indulgence with a genuine, deep love for her family which continued unaltered as long as she lived. Until she was nine, she was educated at home. Apparently her lack of contact with children her own age did not distress her; she was capable even then of creating a world of her own, for she had a vivid imagination. Imagination, sensitivity, and a tendency to court solitude were to be major factors in her poetic achievement, but they were to prove disastrous in personal relationships. The revealing lines in one of her early poems, "Beatrice,"

> For I, who die, could wish that I had lived
> A little closer to the world of men,

were, in a very real sense, prophetic. The solicitude and overprotectiveness of her parents may have been unwise; in their defense it can only be said that they did the best they knew for their daughter at that time. If this isolation from her contemporaries increased her innate shyness, it surely deepened her instinctive awareness of beauty, not only in her surroundings, but also in the written and spoken word. Like all children of such households at that time, she was constantly read to, and in this way she was first introduced to poetry. Her favorite poem was Christina Rossetti's "Christmas Carol": "I think I liked it better than other poems partly because snow is mentioned in it," she said many years later.[11] Snow, light, and especially stars (once she expressed wonderment that there was no star worship, as there was of sun and moon) [12] delighted her, and all these were to become repeated motifs in her poetry. And it was undoubtedly her own experience which led her to compile *Rainbow Gold*, an anthology of poems for children, and to say about it, "A child should enjoy a poem just as he enjoys a ride in an automobile, without needing to understand the mechanism of the machine, and without needing to know what was in the inventor's mind." [13]

When she was nine years old, she was sent for a time to a small private school; [14] then she entered Hosmer Hall, a "young ladies' academy" which had been established for the express purpose of preparing its students to enter college. Here she first encountered the poetry of Sappho and Heinrich Heine, later important influences in her own work; it was also at Hosmer Hall that her own poetic gift was first recognized.[15] She had started writing when she was about eleven, had even had one of her poems published in a religious paper—her parents, reading it, never dreamed that the poet was *their* Sara Teasdale until she showed them the rough copy.[16] But now, she began to write in earnest, emboldened by the encouragement of her teachers and of her first real friends. Sara's shyness did not preclude a gift for friendship, which all who knew her well remember as one of her loveliest qualities.

Following her graduation in 1902, she, with seven other young women (all of whom later made notable achievements in the creative arts) joined in publishing a manuscript magazine which they called *The Potter's Wheel*.[17] Most of the poems which comprised Sara Teasdale's first volume, published in 1907, made their initial appearance in its pages. Stimulated by the congenial, friendly—if competitive—ambiance that "The Potters" provided, she now "took wing." No one living in St. Louis at that time or for many years afterwards, who had any social or cultural connections, could possibly be unaware of this unique group; and, inevitably, an issue of *The Potter's Wheel* came to the attention of William Marion Reedy, one of the giants in

American journalism, who was always alert to new literary talent. In the May 30, 1907, issue of his weekly, *Reedy's Mirror,* he published Sara Teasdale's dramatic monologue "Guenevere." The *Mirror* had a nation-wide following, and the poem attracted considerable notice.[18]

Sara now had the incentive to compile her first volume, and she set painstakingly to work. Interestingly enough, like Amy Lowell, one of her poetic inspirations had been Eleonora Duse; she had never met or seen the actress, but photographs had been enough to evoke a number of sonnets [19] which, though perhaps a trifle over-imbued with schoolgirl "crush" beyond the schoolgirl age, nevertheless hold some arresting lines:

> Your mouth's mute weariness is not despair.
> Perhaps among us craven earth-born things
> God loves its silence better than a prayer.

and,

> Carved in the silence by the hand of Pain,
> And made more perfect by the gift of Peace,
> Than if Delight had bid your sorrow cease,
> And brought the dawn to where the dark has lain,
> And set a smile upon your lips again.

by contemporary testimony do recall the personality of Duse, and indicate that Sara's gift for simple, connotative language was early becoming manifest. And in a little lyric called "The Gift," there is evidence of the poignant understatement which she was ultimately to bring to perfection:

> What shall I give you, my lord, my lover?
> The gift that breaks the heart in me:
> I bid you awake at dawn and discover
> I have gone my way and left you free.

Since at this point in her life there had been no serious "romances"—at least none have been recorded—it may be assumed that the situation depicted in the poem was imaginary. Which leads to the conclusion that, even in her later poetry which was definitely based on personal emotions and experience, also there might be an equally strong imaginative element which makes it impossible to say with certainty whether the poet is speaking in her own voice or not.

"Sonnets to Duse" and Other Poems appeared in the autumn of 1907. It had a very limited distribution, but, in a burst of unusual daring, Sara sent a copy to Arthur Symons, the English critic, because he, too, admired Duse. Her daring—and it was daring for her!—was rewarded by a pleasant notice in the Saturday Review of London, in which Mr. Symons remarked, "This book is a small delightful thing which one is not tempted to say much about, but to welcome." [20] For Sara, however, merely to have received the notice of the great Arthur Symons was accolade enough, and she now felt that she had been given the highest possible encouragement to persevere in her vocation.

But her health was precarious—too much so to permit her to expend her energy as prodigally as she would have liked in writing. She was frailly built and frailly nerved, easily exhausted by overexertion or excitement. She had already begun to live according to a strict regime: so many hours for rest, so many for writing, so many to see her friends who usually arranged special times for their visits.[21] Most people considered this a sensible arrangement, though, inevitably, there were those who considered it rather selfish and arrogant. But for Sara, this self-imposed discipline was a necessary means to an end. Her careful portioning of time was designed to strike just the right balance between the pleasures of friendship, and solitude, even at the risk of concomitant intervening loneliness.[22] The way of life that Sara Teasdale had to live was as necessary for her to accomplish her work as Amy Lowell's "sky parlor," or Emily Dickinson's "smallest room" were for them. Not that she did not give way to occasional moments of rebellion against this regime. The often quoted lines,

> O Beauty, are you not enough?
> Why am I crying after love?

underscore the other side of her nature which her friends knew well—the ardent, vibrant woman, with a tremendous capacity for giving and receiving love, as opposed to one living in self-imposed near-austerity.

Though *Sonnets to Duse* did not have a sensational success, it did bring, among other joys, a valuable and valued friend into Sara's life, Marion Cummings Stanley. Mrs. Stanley, a professor at the University of Arizona, was also a poet. A lengthy correspondence led to Sara's spending the winter of 1908 in Tucson, and the experience was a crucial one for her. Just as the three-month tour of Europe and the Holy Land which she had taken with her mother in 1905 had greatly stimulated her,[23] so that period in Arizona had its liberating, charismatic effect, both professionally and personally. Eighteen years later, in one of her most "confessional" poems, "Day's Ending (Tucson)," she said of that moment of truth,

> It was not long that I lived there
> But I became a woman
> Under those vehement stars,
> For it was there I heard
> For the first time my spirit
> Forging an iron rule for me,
> As though with slow cold hammers
> Beating out word by word:

> "Only yourself can heal you,
> Only yourself can lead you,
> The road is heavy going
> And ends where no man knows;
> Take love when love is given,
> But never think to find it
> A sure escape from sorrow
> Or a complete repose."

Prior to World War I, there was a tremendous market for poetry in the magazines, and between 1908 and 1910, Sara was regularly published in *Putnam's*, *Harper's* and *Scribner's*. She was becoming nationally known, and New York now beckoned.

In January, 1911, she came to the city for the first time; much to her delight her name was put in nomination for the Poetry Society of America. She attended one of the meetings where, as is customary to this day, poems were read aloud and the floor thrown open for a free-for-all discussion. Witter Bynner read Sara's "Helen of Troy;" no record of the ensuing discussion has been preserved, which is unfortunate, for Ezra Pound happened to be in the audience that night.[24] But she was wholeheartedly welcomed; Jessie Rittenhouse, the secretary, became her unofficial sponsor and introduced her to all the great and near-great of the literary world, who were unsparing of their admiration for the poet, even though her poetry might not have been altogether to their taste. She was young, not pretty, but she had the look and bearing of an aristocrat; she wore deliberately simple gowns made of fine fabrics with almost no ornamentation. She looked like a poet, and her modesty was a delightful, refreshing contrast to the volubility of certain ones who, figuratively speaking, carried placards. Without the slightest self-deprecation, she was, nonetheless, genuinely impressed and excited at meeting people who had long been famous.[25]

She left New York regretfully, only to return the next year (1912) following the triumphant publication of *Helen of Troy and Other Poems*. The book had an unequivocal success and was enthusiastically reviewed. She spent the summer in Europe with Jessie Rittenhouse, sight-seeing and writing many of the poems which would appear in her next volume, *Rivers to the Sea*; and when she returned to America that autumn, she received another accolade. Her poem, "I Shall Not Care," had been chosen for publication in *The Lyric Year*, an anthology of contemporary poetry in which it was considered an honor to be represented. The following year, she appeared for the first time in *The Anthology of Magazine Verse*, edited annually by William Stanley Braithwaite of the Boston *Transcript*, which, from its first issue in 1913 to its last in 1929, always included some of her work.

From 1912 on, she began to spend more and more time in

New York, for her circle of friends and acquaintances continued to widen, as her poetry gained in recognition. Among these was John Hall Wheelock, whom she met for the first time in 1913. She had read his *The Human Fantasy* (1911) and *The Belovèd Adventure* (1912) with intense admiration, and had praised him enthusiastically. She said that unequivocally he would be one of America's most distinguished poets, and her judgment proved correct. Mr. Wheelock has published eight volumes of poetry since 1912, and his poems appear in almost all anthologies. He has received many awards, the latest being the Bollingen Prize in 1962. Sara's friendship with him began, as her friendships so often did, through letters. He had read *Helen of Troy*, liked it, and had written to tell her so; she had responded with grateful appreciation, and, learning that he worked at Scribner's Book Store, she deliberately made a point of stopping by to meet him. "A rather surprising thing, considering how shy she was," he recalled later,[26] but poets were "special" to her, and deserving of extraordinary gestures. During her 1913 visit to New York, their relationship grew into one of deep affection, rooted primarily in the genuine love of poetry which they both completely shared. To the end of her life, John Hall Wheelock was Sara Teasdale's cherished friend and unofficial advisor; it is interesting to note her frank statement to the effect that she was first attracted to the man whom she eventually married because he so much resembled Mr. Wheelock, not only in appearance, but in spirit and understanding as well.

For despite her conviction that beauty should be enough for her—a conviction that John Hall Wheelock made no effort to disturb—and that beauty and poetry quite fulfilled her secret dreams, she was learning that she could not deny her very human need for love. In 1913 during a brief visit to Chicago, rival of New York as a literary mecca, she had met Harriet Monroe. Miss Monroe wanted Vachel Lindsay to meet Sara, but he was not in the city at that time; Sara had already read some of his poetry, however, and had then written him a congratulatory letter. (One of her most delightful characteristics

Emily Dickinson

Amy Lowell

Edna St. Vincent Millay

Sara Teasdale, aged six

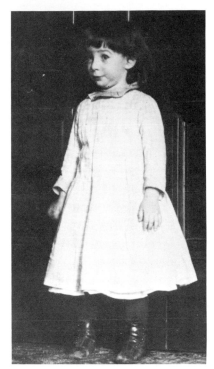

COURTESY OF JOHN HALL WHEELOCK

Sara Teasdale, aged nine

COURTESY OF
JOHN HALL WHEELOCK

*Sara Teasdale
in her early twenties*

COURTESY OF JOHN HALL WHEELOCK

PHOTOGRAPH BY RICHARD AVEDON

Marianne Moore

was her honest pleasure at reading any poetry that she considered "near perfection," whatever its genre; [27] and invariably she would write the poet of her appreciation, whether they had met or not.) Lindsay admired her poetry, too, and he was even more intrigued by what he had heard about her. By the time he called upon her at her parents' home in St. Louis in February, 1914,[28] he was well on his way to falling in love with her—the resemblance of Sara Teasdale to Elizabeth Barrett had already been commented on by several of her friends, and Lindsay was by no means loath to cast himself in the role of Robert Browning. He was a strong, vital man, with a delightful sense of humor, and an energetic enthusiasm which carried all before it. He rushed into Sara's life like a passionate tempest, courting her with long, ardent letters, bewildering, and, for a time, almost bemusing her.

She knew long before he did how deeply he loved her; frightened, but at the same time excited by the torrent of feeling that his pursuit aroused in her, she seriously considered marrying him. Rationally she knew that such a course might be disastrous to them both, but emotionally she was still "crying after love" which this vibrant poet was pouring out to her. She had never met anyone quite like him. She knew his circumstances—he was utterly frank with her—and they offered none of the stability to which she had been accustomed from the day she was born. Vachel Lindsay had broken completely with his family, and chose to travel, finding the inspiration for his poetry in hiking all over America, doing odd jobs as he found them in return for food and shelter. He refused to take on any kind of obligation that might inhibit his freedom; even engagements for poetry readings, at which he excelled, he accepted reluctantly and only when he was in dire need of money. Certainly prudence would caution a young woman as sheltered as Sara Teasdale not even to encourage such a suitor, much less take him seriously, but she could not in honesty deny that she found his need for her affection very appealing. And the relationship meant much to her as a poet, for they read each other's work and criticized it freely. Lindsay admitted that the lady in his exquisite poem "The Chinese Nightingale" was herself, and no woman—poet or not—could be immune to such a tribute.

Her indecision increased the more because there was another man who possessed every quality she could wish for in a husband, including the stability which Lindsay so conspicuously lacked. He was not a poet. His name was Ernst Filsinger, and he was a substantial St. Louis business man. Sara met him in April, 1914, not through letters but very socially at the home of a mutual friend. Tall, dark, distinguished looking, a gentle man as well as a gentleman, he had loved Sara devotedly from afar ever since he had read "Sonnets to Duse," revealing a romantic quality which Sara could not fail to appreciate. Like John Hall Wheelock, he had the high ideals that she admired in a man; like Vachel Lindsay, he was capable of great ardor. There was no doubt of his ability to take care of her, nor of his eagerness to do so. Above all, he understood the refinement and fastidiousness that were bred into her bones, and appreciated both. Ernst Filsinger was the kind of man who automatically put women on pedestals, and the highest one was reserved for Sara Teasdale. He was proud of her, he wanted her to continue to write poetry and was willing to adjust his life to hers.

Sara's inner turmoil and indecision were intense. The difficulty was that both Vachel Lindsay and Ernst Filsinger were good men by her most idealistic standards. The question was which one would make her the better husband, and—a consideration which certainly entered her thoughts—for which one would she make the best wife? Lindsay was prepared to sacrifice his "freedom" but should she permit it? Might it not endanger his work? How long could he be happy with her, before he would chafe at the restrictions which marriage would inevitably impose upon him? Could she face the prospect of living in near-poverty? Would it not be better for him to give him the gift she had so long ago proffered her imaginary lover, and left him free? Ernst Filsinger loved her devotedly, and she admired and respected him. He was not a whirlwind, but whirlwinds could be exhausting. Lindsay's dynamism was delightful in small doses, but living with it could be difficult, especially if they both happened to become temperamental about their work at the same time! And while everyone she knew was fond of Lindsay, when it came to marriage, opinion of family and friends—however subtly expressed—was heavily weighted in favor of Ernst Filsinger. In the end, her own fundamental common sense prevailed, and she accepted Ernst's proposal.

Informing Vachel Lindsay of her decision must have been extremely difficult for her; fortunately he was not disposed to be angry or vindictive. Honorably he destroyed all the letters she had written him, and congratulated Ernst Filsinger. He remained Sara's devoted friend, and later became a firm friend of her husband's as well—strong indication that, in his own opinion at least, it was simply a matter of the better man having won. That Sara's feeling for him had been, and continued to be, deep and completely honest, was revealed in her poem "In Memory of Vachel Lindsay," published in her posthumous volume *Strange Victory:*

"Deep in the ages," you said, "deep in the ages,"
    And, "To live in mankind is far more than to live in a name."
You are deep in the ages, now, deep in the ages,
    You whom the world could not break, nor the years tame.

Fly out, fly on, eagle that is not forgotten,
    Fly straight to the innermost light, you who loved sun in your
                                                    eyes,
Free of the fret, free of the weight of living,
    Bravest among the brave, gayest among the wise.

A tribute (together with Lindsay's letters to her, and to others of his friends) which does much to exonerate Sara of the charge sometimes made against her—that she deliberately toyed with his affections and then broke his heart.

Radiantly happy, Sara married Ernst Filsinger at her parents' home on December 18, 1914, surrounded by both completely approving families. For all her poetic temperament, she was,

after all, a Teasdale of St. Louis, and fully imbued with the
attitudes towards marriage that a young woman of her class
and upbringing instinctively observed. Ernst was the kind of
husband she would have chosen had she not been a poet; this
factor may have been the decisive one in his favor. They went
to Boston for their honeymoon, then on to New York so that
Ernst could meet her friends, all of whom were delighted at
the marriage. The young couple's love for each other was manifest to all beholders, and it seemed that the princess had indeed
married Prince Charming. No one doubted that their life together would be a happy one.

Most unfortunately, however, this happiness was not destined
to last. The conflict within Sara Teasdale between an inherent
need for giving and receiving love, and an equally imperative
need for solitude in which to think and work, could be subdued
for a time, but not indefinitely. Nor did she find love "A sure
escape from sorrow/Or a complete repose." Her husband did
everything humanly possible to smooth the way for her, and
it is certainly true that during this time she wrote some of her
finest poetry: *Rivers to the Sea* (1915); *Love Songs* (1917)
which went through five editions and won the Columbia-Poetry
Society of America Prize; *Flame and Shadow* (1920); and *Dark
of the Moon* (1926). She also published *The Answering Voice*
(1917), an anthology of love poems written by women, and her
collection of poetry for children, *Rainbow Gold* (1922). Ernst
Filsinger was as understanding of the demands of her life as his
experience, and limitations, could make him. When they were
invited to social functions which he enjoyed attending, she
frequently preferred not to go; he willingly made excuses for
her non-appearance, saying that "she was not very well and
did not go out much, but that she was a rare and beautiful
spirit." [29] To him she was the sun and moon and starlight, but
never the firelight—which in marriage is sometimes essential.
He had a genuine passion for poetry and he knew all her poems
by heart, though Sara did not usually enjoy hearing him recite
them because she found his delivery over-sentimental.[30] He

could not, however, easily understand that the writing of poetry meant almost life itself to her.

There is no doubt that Sara loved him devotedly, but it is possible that very early in her marriage she began to wonder whether she might not be a better poet if she were not a wife as well.

> For with my singing I can make
> A refuge for my spirit's sake,
> A house of shining words, to be
> My fragile immortality.

And that refuge became so necessary to her that, more and more, it was a refuge not only spiritually, but emotionally and physically as well. Her need for it, real or imagined, played havoc with her life. She shrank into herself more and more; when Ernst's many business interests required that he travel to Europe or to South America, she felt that she could not accompany him and remained at home, fearing to be a detriment to his activities. Despite their love and actual need for each other, they inevitably drifted farther and farther apart, and misunderstandings frequently arose, all the more devastating because their dispositions had seemed to mesh so well in the beginning. Ernst seemed now, Sara thought, to live only for his business. Never having had similar demands made upon her, she was really quite naively unaware that his attention to his work was truly necessary, if he was to survive in the chaotic post-war world. Though she made little complaint, it is possible that she began to resent his lengthy absences. Ernst, too, albeit unintentionally and unconsciously, may have displayed impatience with her, not realizing that his interest in her accomplishment was as important to her, as hers was to him. A perpetual *princesse lointaine* would find the role of a wife difficult to play, and the emotional strain that Sara was now experiencing began to reveal itself in her poetry:

> Earth is hostile and the sea hostile,
>   Why do I look for a place to rest?

I must fight always and die fighting
    With fear an unhealing wound in my breast.

The buoyant excitement of her earlier work is gone; a somber
note is struck in *Flame and Shadow*—"My heart is a garden,
tired with autumn." Surely in the poem called "Change" is
found a most poignant expression of her feelings during this
time:

Remember me as I was then;
    Turn from me now, but always see
The laughing shadowy girl who stood
    At midnight by the flowering tree,
With eyes that love had made as bright
As the trembling stars of the summer night.

Turn from me now, but always hear
    The muted laughter in the dew
Of that one year of youth we had,
    The only youth we ever knew—
Turn from me now, or you will see
What other years have done to me.

Once again she thought a "gift" seemed to be demanded of
her. She tried to talk to her husband about a divorce, but he,
immeasurably shocked, refused. He adored her; the thought of
losing her was horrifying. With this impasse Sara existed for a
time, but by late summer of 1929, she could stand it no longer.
Ernst was abroad on a business trip. According to Margaret
Conklin, literary executor of her estate, "She wrote him a long
letter, explaining her unshakable decision to obtain a divorce
and speaking warmly of their early happy years together;" [31]
then, without telling her plans to any but a very few close
friends, she went to Reno to obtain her decree which was
granted without contest on September 5. [32] The experience was
a shattering one for her, but she had determined that this must
be—that *he* must be set free from a bond that no longer
brought him happiness. It is impossible not to conclude that
her action, at this crucial moment, was motivated largely by

over-sensitivity which brought on brooding over occurrences far less important than they actually were, what the present generation would call "over-reacting." By all testimony, Sara had no reason to doubt Ernst Filsinger's love for her; when he received her letter, he was heartbroken, though he made no effort to change her intent. As for Sara, the foreboding lines she had written three years earlier in *Dark of the Moon* (even the title of the volume is significant for a poet who had always been entranced by moonlight) were fulfilled to the uttermost—even to the September day:

> I have no heart for any other joy,
>   The drenched September day turns to depart,
> And I have said good-bye to what I love;
>   With my own will I vanquished my own heart.
>
> On the long wind I hear the winter coming,
>   The window panes are cold and blind with rain;
> With my own will I turned the summer from me
>   And summer will not come to me again.

Her dramatic, poet's "gift" had brought genuine human tragedy, from which neither she nor Ernst Filsinger ever wholly recovered.

She no longer needed to seek for solitude. Now her life was filled with loneliness. Many of her friends whom she had loved devotedly had left New York; some of them had died. She tried valiantly to carry on as before, but her spiritual solace had not sufficient religious depth to sustain her through this crisis. She might have become a complete recluse, had it not been for John Hall Wheelock, who called and telephoned frequently; Vachel Lindsay (now married) who came to see her whenever he was in New York; and Margaret Conklin, who was in the editorial department of Macmillan's, Sara's publishers. Their relationship, which Sara described as rather like that of a mother to a daughter [33]—not because of age, but because of wisdom and understanding—brought her happiness and great comfort. A few, new friends came to see her, too, always at her behest on a stated day at a stated time. To one of them, Margery Mansfield, then secretary of the Poetry Society of America, she said one day, quite unexpectedly, that "poetry always failed you when you needed it most." [34] Was this her admission that the freedom which she had sacrificed everything to possess had also failed her?

That she decided to work for a time in prose is significant. At first she considered doing a study of childhood in ancient Greece,[35] but soon discovered that the research would be too difficult and might not net enough material for an entire book. It was in this emotionally depleted state that word reached her on December 5, 1931, of Vachel Lindsay's suicide. As John Hall Wheelock has written, "The impact of this shock shook her to the roots." [36] Poetry, in which she had always found surcease for emotional turmoil had, at least temporarily, "failed her." Yet it was in work alone that she could find comfort, if there was any to be found.

She began seriously to consider doing a biography of Christina Rossetti, the poet she had loved so much as a child, and had continued to love over the years. In the summer of 1932, she went to England to do research; the interest her publishers took in this project encouraged her greatly, and by the time she reached London in June she was genuinely excited over it. At first everything went according to plan, but in August, in one of the treacherous changes of English climate, she took cold, which quickly turned to pneumonia. She refused to enter a hospital there and insisted upon returning home—later the ship's doctor said that he did not see how she could have survived the voyage.[37] The doctors she consulted in America warned her that she had been critically ill and must rest, because in addition to possible damage to her lungs, she had a heart murmur and abnormally high blood pressure. At this news, she was terrified. She consulted numerous doctors, but none could give her any help. Her physical weakness and acute depression increased, as she finally forced herself to realize that there was no possibility of her getting well.

Quietly she set her affairs in order. Margery Mansfield tells how, in mid-January, 1933, she received an unexpected telephone call from Sara who told her—much to her surprise and pleasure—how highly she had valued their friendship and how much she appreciated all that she had done for her.[38] At the time, Miss Mansfield considered it only the lovely, graceful gesture of a lonely friend. Later, when the manner of Sara's death was announced—that her nurse had come into the bedroom at the usual hour, and, not finding her patient there, had gone into the adjoining bathroom and found her lying in a tub of still warm water—the phone call became quite understandable. Sara had taken a large dose of the sedation prescribed for her, counting on slipping wholly into the water after she became unconscious. Miss Mansfield writes, "Such a phone call would be like her. With her extremely conscientious nature she would ask, will anyone be hurt by this, and can I do anything to prevent it? I don't want innocent people blaming themselves for it, or feeling they have failed." [39] And she, like Sara's other friends, once they had recovered from the shock of her death, felt without exception, that it had provided a merciful release.

"Suffering and experience uncovered in this gentlest of human beings a vein of iron, an inner strength that enables her to speak to us in the accents of great poetry," John Hall Wheelock has said of Sara Teasdale.[40] There are two kinds of poetry that achieve greatness. One is that which deliberately explores the great fundamentals of human experience, which attains its universality, no matter what its origin in time and space, simply because it *is* concerned with elemental issues which are instantly recognizable. The drama of life, love, sin, salvation, redemption in a Shakespeare play or an Homeric epic, or a study of the world like *The Canterbury Tales*, literally seizes the reader intellectually, as well as emotionally, and forces him to recognize his own personal moment of truth when the protagonists of the literary work recognize theirs. But there is another kind of poetry that can quite as validly be called great—that poetry which begins with a deeply felt, uniquely personal emotion, yet at the same time is set down so objectively that the poem is not merely an extension of the poet, but stands as an entity by itself. Sara Teasdale once said that no one could tell from a poet's work what he will actually be like.[41] This statement is perhaps a warning to readers not to take even a Teasdale poem as a literal, verbatim transcription of her life. As Professor Bartlett Giamatti has remarked, "Love poets are often, I suspect, far more interested . . . in writing poetry than in making love . . . Poems are the real children of love poets." [42]

Sara Teasdale obviously shared the view that the poet's task is to bring the imperfect to perfection, the chaotic into structure and order. Her reading of Emily Dickinson certainly influenced her; there are definite similarities to be found in their stanzaic patterns, and she herself once affirmed that "reading Emily Dickinson would help any poet's technique." [43] Not that her poetry is of uniform excellence; many poems, especially the early ones, can be justly criticized for over-sentimentality, and for describing, rather than evoking, emotion. But when she was at her best, as in *Dark of the Moon* and *Strange Victory*, the beautiful craftsmanship which was the distinctive quality of her poetry, was matched by an equally beautiful austerity and economy of language.

She said little about the craft of poetry, but what she did say was, as might be expected, highly subjective. Like Emily Dickinson, she would not lay down any hard and fast rules.

> My theory is that poems are written because of a state of emotional irritation. It may be present for some time before the poet is conscious of what is tormenting him . . . A poem springs from emotions produced by an actual experience, or almost as forcefully from those produced by an imaginary experience. In either case, the poem is written to free the poet from an emotional burden.[44]

It is not surprising to discover that frequently her poems were not written down until they had been in her mind for a long time, and, once written, seldom needed altering. As she said herself, "A poem of the type I write is so brief and simple, there

isn't much that revision can do for it; either it has something
or it doesn't. If it doesn't, I simply throw it away." [45] She recognized the need for this period of contemplation between the
immediate inspiration and the final work, in order to retain
that objective view of the "emotional burden" which would
make the reader respond, without the presence of the poet in-
truding on that response.

By shaping his poem with perfect exactitude to hold his emotion,
he fulfills his subconscious aim in composition. He sets himself
free by pouring his thought into a form which holds it completely
and in which he can contemplate it as a thing apart from himself.[46]

At the same time, she knew what this exactitude demanded:

> I lived with the swift singing strength of fire,
> Seeking for beauty as a flame for fuel—
> Beauty in all things and in every hour.
> The gods have given life—I gave them song;
> The debt is paid, and now I turn to go.

To give beauty "*song*"—i.e., words—was the vocation of few,
and the price was high:

> Life you have put me in your debt
>   And I must serve you long—
> But oh, the debt is terrible
>   That must be paid in song.

But there were moments of triumph:

> From my spirit's gray defeat,
> From my pulse's flagging beat,
> From my hopes that turned to sand
> Sifting through my close-clenched hand,
> From my own fault's slavery,
> If I can sing, I still am free.

Though love in all its facets is the major theme of her poetry,
wild, epic passion finds no place in it. She was no Emily Brontë

or Christina Rossetti. Even when writing of such women as Guenevere or Maria Alcoforando, where wild bursts of emotion might be expected, we find characteristically restrained simplicity in the depths of despair—for example, in the opening lines of "Guenevere":

> I was a queen, and I have lost my crown;
> A wife, and I have broken all my vows;
> A lover, and I ruined him I loved:—
> There is no other havoc left to do.

This passage conveys fully the sense of futility demanded by the situation, and is the more effective for its lack of histrionics. Sara Teasdale knew that the deepest emotions seldom find utterance: "Those who love the most, Do not talk of their love," one poem begins, and the second stanza gives one of those exquisite vignettes at which she excelled:

> And a woman I used to know
> Who loved one man from her youth,
> Against the strength of the fates
> Fighting in somber pride,
> Never spoke of this thing,
> But hearing his name by chance,
> A light would pass over her face.

In the poem, "Appraisal," she put into words what many have realized, but could never express so perceptively, with a touch of humor—completely without malice—that is delightful.

> Never think she loves him wholly,
> Never believe her love is blind,
> All his faults are locked securely
> In a closet of her mind;
> All his indecisions folded
> Like old flags that time has faded,
> Limp and streaked with rain,
> And his cautiousness like garments
> Frayed and thin, with many a stain—

Let them be, oh let them be,
There is treasure to outweigh them,
His proud will that sharply stirred,
Climbs as surely as the tide,
Senses strained too taut to sleep,
Gentleness to beast and bird,
Humor flickering hushed and wide
As the moon on moving water,
And a tenderness too deep
To be gathered in a word.

Her "Advice to a Girl" is a miracle of compression, sum-
ming up in thirteen lines what marriage counselors, taking
twice as many hours, are seldom able to convey:

No one worth possessing
Can be quite possessed;
Lay that on your heart,
My young angry dear;
This truth, this hard and precious stone,
Lay it on your hot cheek,
Let it hide your tear.
Hold it like a crystal
When you are alone
And gaze in the depths of the icy stone.
Look, look long and you will be blessed:
No one worth possessing
Can be quite possessed.

The ability to transmit bitter experience without bitterness,
and to laugh wisely, was one which Sara Teasdale possessed in
the highest degree.

Nevertheless, when all is said and done, there is still a quality
in her work which defies analysis. Her poetry does not lend
itself to a frantic search for ambiguities or provide a forest for
symbol hunters. It depends greatly for its impact upon the
reader's empathy and imaginative response; it is not an intellectual exercise, but an experience. Like herself, her poetry is at
times elusive, impossible to categorize, and therein lies its fas-

cination and charm. To quote Oscar Williams, "She's an irritating creature! How can you write a learned exegesis about a poem like 'The Coin,' for instance? It's all there—and it's marvellous. What more can anyone say?" One more thing might be said, however. Sara Teasdale did not become the song she sang; she *was* that song:

> I should be glad of loneliness
>   And hours that go on broken wings,
> A thirsty body, a tired heart
>   And the unchanging ache of things,
> If I could make a single song
>   As lovely and as full of light,
> As hushed and brief as a falling star
>   On a winter night.

And, though contemporary critics have tended to neglect her, thousands of others testify that, even in the cynical Sixties, her "single songs" are still lovely and still full of light, and still bring joy and often comfort to the heart. Which was all that she herself ever hoped or asked.

Footnotes

Most of the material relating to Sara Teasdale and Vachel Lindsay is restricted, either under copyright provision by previous biographers, or, in the case of Lindsay, by the projected definitive edition of his letters to be done by Norman Holmes Pearson of Yale University, which the world eagerly awaits. Readers presently in search of further information about these two poets are therefore referred to *Sara Teasdale: A Biography*, by Margaret Haley Carpenter, and *The West-Going Heart*, a biography of Vachel Lindsay, by Eleanor Ruggles.

Poems are from *The Collected Poems of Sara Teasdale*, Macmillan, 1966.

[1] Sara Teasdale, unfinished ms. biography of Christina Rossetti, quoted by permission of Margaret Conklin, literary executor of Miss Teasdale's estate.

[2] Howard Willard Cook, *Our*

Poets of Today (Moffat, Yard & Co., 1918), 14.

3 John Hall Wheelock, conversation with author.

4 Margaret Conklin, letter to author.

5 Wheelock, "Sara Teasdale," ms. property of author.

6 "Sara Teasdale," brochure published by Macmillan Co., *c.* 1927.

7 Wheelock ms.

8 *Ibid.*

9 Wheelock, conversation with author.

10 *Ibid.*

11 Macmillan brochure

12 Margery Mansfield, "Conversations with Sara Teasdale," ms., property of author.

13 Macmillan brochure

14 Wheelock ms.

15 *Ibid.*

16 Mansfield ms.

17 Macmillan brochure

18 Wheelock, conversation with author.

19 *Ibid.*

20 *Saturday Review*, October 5, 1907.

21 Mansfield ms. Miss Mansfield's time was Thursday afternoon.

22 *Ibid.*

23 Wheelock ms.

24 For such details as are available, cf Jessie Rittenhouse, *My House of Life*, Houghton Mifflin, 1934, 228–29. Conduct of Poetry Society meetings from personal knowledge.

25 Wheelock, conversation with author.

26 *Ibid.*

27 Conklin, letter to author.

28 Wheelock ms.

29 Mansfield ms.

30 Wheelock, conversation with and letter to author.

31 Conklin, notation to author.

32 Wheelock ms.

33 Mansfield ms.

34 *Ibid.*

35 *Ibid.*

36 Wheelock, letter to author.

37 Wheelock, conversation with author.

38 Mansfield ms.

39 *Ibid.*

40 Wheelock, letter to author.

41 Mansfield ms.

42 Bartlett Giamatti, "Dante and Love," lecture given at the Dante Symposium, University of San Francisco, August, 1968.

43 Mansfield ms.

44 Marguerite Wilkinson, *The Way of the Makers* (Macmillan, 1925), 260.

45 Mansfield ms.

46 Wilkinson, 261.

Poems

The Metropolitan Tower

We walked together in the dusk
    To watch the tower grow dimly white,
And saw it lift against the sky
    Its flower of amber light.

You talked of half a hundred things,
    I kept each hurried word you said;
And when at last the hour was full,
    I saw the light turn red.

You did not know the time had come,
    You did not see the sudden flower,
Nor know that in my heart Love's birth
    Was reckoned from that hour.

The Kiss

I hoped that he would love me,
    And he has kissed my mouth,
But I am like a stricken bird
    That cannot reach the south.

For though I know he loves me,
    To-night my heart is sad;
His kiss was not so wonderful
    As all the dreams I had.

A Winter Night

My window-pane is starred with frost,
     The world is bitter cold to-night,
The moon is cruel, and the wind
     Is like a two-edged sword to smite.

God pity all the homeless ones,
     The beggars pacing to and fro,
God pity all the poor to-night
     Who walk the lamp-lit streets of snow.

My room is like a bit of June,
     Warm and close-curtained fold on fold,
But somewhere, like a homeless child,
     My heart is crying in the cold.

The Look

Strephon kissed me in the spring,
     Robin in the fall,
But Colin only looked at me
     And never kissed at all.

Strephon's kiss was lost in jest,
     Robin's lost in play,
But the kiss in Colin's eyes
     Haunts me night and day.

Spring Night

The park is filled with night and fog,
     The veils are drawn about the world,

The drowsy lights along the paths
     Are dim and pearled.

Gold and gleaming the empty streets,
     Gold and gleaming the misty lake,
The mirrored lights like sunken swords,
     Glimmer and shake

Oh, is it not enough to be
Here with this beauty over me?
My throat should ache with praise, and I
Should kneel in joy beneath the sky.
O, beauty are you not enough?
Why am I crying after love,
With youth, a singing voice and eyes
To take earth's wonder with surprise?
Why have I put off my pride,
Why am I unsatisfied,—
I for whom the pensive night
Binds her cloudy hair with light,—
I for whom all beauty burns
Like incense in a million urns?
O, beauty, are you not enough?
Why am I crying after love?

The Answer

When I go back to earth
And all my joyous body
Puts off the red and white
That once had been so proud,
If men should pass above
With false and feeble pity,
My dust will find a voice
To answer them aloud:

"Be still, I am content,
Take back your poor compassion,
Joy was a flame in me
Too steady to destroy;
Lithe as a bending reed
Loving the storm that sways her—
I found more joy in sorrow
Than you could find in joy."

Riches

I have no riches but my thoughts,
    Yet these are wealth enough for me;
My thoughts of you are golden coins
    Stamped in the mint of memory;

And I must spend them all in song,
    For thoughts, as well as gold, must be
Left on the hither side of death
    To gain their immortality.

Barter

Life has loveliness to sell,
    All beautiful and splendid things,
Blue waves whitened on a cliff,
    Soaring fire that sways and sings,
And children's faces looking up
Holding wonder like a cup.

Life has loveliness to sell,
    Music like a curve of gold,
Scent of pine trees in the rain,
    Eyes that love you, arms that hold,

And for your spirit's still delight,
Holy thoughts that star the night.

Spend all you have for loveliness,
 Buy it and never count the cost;
For one white singing hour of peace
 Count many a year of strife well lost,
And for a breath of ecstasy
Give all you have been, or could be.

Wisdom

When I have ceased to break my wings
Against the faultiness of things,
And learned that compromises wait
Behind each hardly opened gate,
When I can look Life in the eyes,
Grown calm and very coldly wise,
Life will have given me the Truth,
And taken in exchange—my youth.

Stars

Alone in the night
 On a dark hill
With pines around me
 Spicy and still,

And a heaven full of stars
 Over my head,
White and topaz
 And misty red;

Myriads with beating
 Hearts of fire

That aeons
  Cannot vex or tire;

Up the dome of heaven
  Like a great hill,
I watch them marching
  Stately and still,

And I know that I
  Am honored to be
Witness
  Of so much majesty.

"What Do I Care?"

What do I care, in the dreams and the languor of spring,
  That my songs do not show me at all?
For they are a fragrance, and I am a flint and a fire,
  I am an answer, they are only a call.

But what do I care, for love will be over so soon,
  Let my heart have its say and my mind stand idly by,
For my mind is proud and strong enough to be silent,
  It is my heart that makes my songs, not I.

The Wine

I cannot die, who drank delight
  From the cup of the crescent moon,
And hungrily as men eat bread,
  Loved the scented nights of June.

The rest may die—but is there not
  Some shining strange escape for me
Who sought in Beauty the bright wine
  Of immortality?

The Coin

Into my heart's treasury
I slipped a coin
That time cannot take
Nor a thief purloin,—
Oh, better than the minting
Of a gold-crowned king
Is the safe-kept memory
Of a lovely thing.

The Beloved

It is enough of honor for one lifetime
To have known you better than the rest have known,
The shadows and the colors of your voice,
Your will, immutable and still as stone.

The shy heart, so lonely and so gay,
The sad laughter and the pride of pride,
The tenderness, the depth of tenderness
Rich as the earth, and wide as heaven is wide.

The Crystal Gazer

I shall gather myself into myself again
I shall take my scattered selves and make them one,
Fusing them into a polished crystal ball
Where I can see the moon and the flashing sun.

I shall sit like a sibyl, hour after hour intent,
Watching the future come and the present go,
And the little shifting pictures of people rushing
In restless self-importance to and fro.

Night

Stars over snow
    And in the west a planet
Swinging below a star—
    Look for a lovely thing and you will find it,
It is not far—
    It never will be far.

Wisdom

Oh to relinquish, with no more of sound
Than the bent bough's when the bright apples fall;
Oh to let go, without a cry or call
That can be heard by any above ground;
Let the dead know, but not the living see—
The dead who loved me will not suffer, knowing
It is all one, the coming or the going,
If I have kept the last, essential me.
If that is safe, then I am safe indeed,
It is my citadel, my church, my home,
My mother and my child, my constant friend;
It is my music, making for my need
A paean like the cymbals of the foam,
Or silence, level, spacious, without end.

Secret Treasure

Fear not that my music seems
Like water locked in winter streams;
You are the sun that many a time

Thawed those rivers into rhyme,
But let them for a while remain
A hidden music in my brain.

Unmeaning phrase and wordless measure,
That unencumbered loveliness
Which is a poet's secret treasure
Sings in me now, and sings no less
That even for your lenient eyes
It will not live in written guise.

"There Will Be Rest"

There will be rest, and sure stars shining
        Over the roof-tops crowned with snow,
A reign of rest, serene forgetting,
        The music of stillness holy and low.

I will make this world of my devising
        Out of a dream in my lonely mind,
I shall find the crystals of peace,—above me
        Stars I shall find.

Last Prelude

If this shall be the last time
The melody flies upward
With its rush of sparks in flight,
Let me go with it in fire and laughter,
Or let me drown if need be
Lost in the swirl of light.
The violins are tuning, whimpering, catching thunder
From the suppressed dark agony of viols—
Once more let heaven clutch me, plunge me under
Miles on uncounted miles.

Edna St. Vincent Millay

1892-1950

*. . . I am not a tentative person. Whatever I do,
I give my whole self to it; and it may be a trial—
most things are, I suppose—but I am never
conscious of making a trial; I am conscious only
of doing the thing that I love to do—that I
have to do.*[1]

*H*AD a foreign visitor to the United States in the mid-1930's
asked the question, "Who is the most popular poet here?" there
could have been only one answer. Actually, the question would
not have needed to be asked, because throughout the world it
was generally known that the answer would be "Edna St. Vincent Millay." From 1912, when "Renascence" catapulted her
into the literary world, until 1944 when a serious illness prevented her writing for nearly two years, hers was a name to
conjure with. Her elegantly slim volumes appeared almost annually from 1917 on, and were eagerly anticipated, bought, and
quoted by her ardent admirers who numbered in the tens of
thousands. And she was acclaimed by the critics as well. Only
when World War II brought her to use poetry for the sake of
propaganda—as she felt, in conscience, that she must do—did
she suffer any critical disparagement; and even this did not
prevent the Poetry Society of America from awarding her its
Gold Medal in 1943 for "meritorious work and abiding interest
in the humanities." [2]

Those fortunate enough to have been in the audience at one
of her poetry readings will never forget her striking appearance
on stage—a slender young woman with shoulder-length tawny
hair, wearing a velvet gown frequently in a shade of burgundy
or deep rose, which made her resemble a figure from a medieval
tapestry. Hearers sat spellbound, listening to a vibrant voice
which gave to words a life that the printed page could not convey; even more fascinating was to watch the poet's face and

137

figure change in interpretation from princess to slut at the lift of an eyebrow or twist of the lips, the movement of a hand or turn of the head. Her readings were performances, in the highest sense of that term. Above all, audiences of any sensitivity at all could sense her integrity and dedication, as well as her giftedness and perception. She was obviously one who had known early what her vocation would be, and had worked with diligence and devotion to scale the heights of her particular mountain.

Not that Vincent Millay (few people called her Edna) was born with a pen in her hand. During her childhood and teens, her ambition was equally divided between becoming a poet and becoming a concert pianist. She had a great musical gift and she worked hard to develop it; to the end of her life two pianos stood in the living room of her home, Steepletop, and she found challenge as well as relaxation in attempting to conquer the most formidable works of Bach and Beethoven. As a student at Vassar, and later during her first years in Greenwich Village, the theatre also claimed her; at Vassar she wrote and played the leading role in *The Princess Marries the Page*, and she became one of the most popular members of the Provincetown Players. Even when she finally decided to be a poet, music and theatre remained strong second loves. It is doubtful that she would have made such a success of her reading tours had she not been exposed to the theatre; or that the Metropolitan Opera Company would have concurred with Deems Taylor's choice of her, out of all American poets then writing, to be librettist for his *The King's Henchman*, had she not been a superlative musician. And both music and drama permeate her poetry—indeed, everything she knew or was capable of doing sooner or later found its way into her work.

She was also, like Emily Dickinson and Amy Lowell, one of the poets who never forgot her childhood. Perhaps this constant overtone of memory is due to the fact that all three were New Englanders, and New Englanders have an inborn habit of harking back to their roots. Vincent Millay was born in Rockland, Maine, on February 22, 1892. She was the eldest child; her younger sisters, Norma and Kathleen, were born in 1893 and 1896, and their very close relationship was due to more than just closeness in age. Their father, a high school teacher and later a school superintendent in Union, Maine, where the family moved when Vincent was still an infant, was also a compulsive gambler, and was divorced from their mother in 1900. Divorce at this time was regarded as highly improper, and a divorced woman was automatically suspect. Cora Millay, left in this situation with three small daughters to support, was fortunately a woman of courage and ingenuity. She was already highly regarded as a practical nurse; in 1903 when she moved her family to Camden, a larger town with greater opportunities, her services were quickly in greater demand. Often she was called away on cases for weeks at a time. Vincent was then put in charge of the household; certainly she learned early about responsibility, especially when finances were undependable, and food sometimes sparse. Yet, shortly before her death, Vincent wrote that her "childhood and girlhood had . . . been so extraordinarily happy." [3] Child psychologists who insist upon tangible "security" in a child's early years must find this comment extraordinary.

Still, there was security in that household, for, despite the divorce, there was no visible bitterness. Henry Millay continued to be interested in and proud of his daughters; when he was seriously ill in 1912, Vincent stayed with her father. And Cora Millay managed to keep unhappiness at a minimum by doing everything possible to keep her daughters from realizing how genuinely poor they sometimes were. She herself had taken singing lessons as a girl, so music—an integral part of her own life—became an integral part of her family's. If there had to be a choice between concert tickets and a new dress, the choice was always in favor of the concert, even though there might not be quite enough fuel for the stoves, either. Cora Millay loved to read, and she inculcated the same avid love of books in her daughters. Vincent had read all of Shakespeare by the

time she was nine; Tennyson, Milton, and the Elizabethan
poets *in toto* by the time she was twelve. What books she did
not find on the Millay bookshelves—and they were numerous—
she obtained at the town library. She started to read Latin poetry before she learned to translate Latin, simply because she
loved the sound of it; in later years she frequently turned to
Latin literature for relaxation, and a volume of Catullus always
traveled with her.

She did not only read poetry, she memorized it. This is not
as unusual a thing as it might seem, for at the turn of the
century when Vincent Millay went to school, "speaking pieces"
and "elocution" were important items in the curriculum. All
across the United States, a special time was set apart each
week, usually the last class hour on Friday, for students to give
recitations. It was the age of the student salutatory and valedic-
tory address, the debating society, the class poem, and formal
instruction in oratory. Sometimes extra memorization was im-
posed as a penalty, a practice upon which the present instruc-
tional method frowns. There was, however, the episode—still
spoken of with amused admiration by graduates of an Indiana
high school—when a student was required as a "punishment"
to recite Bryant's "Thanatopsis," not only to his class but
before the entire school. The student turned penalty into
triumph by literally declaiming the poem, and electrified the
audience into thunderous applause. In this ambience, Vincent
Millay was completely at home. She acted in school plays, many
of which she wrote herself, and, occasionally, was selected by a
touring company manager to play a minor part in a professional
production during its Camden engagement. Her ability was—
if, at first, grudgingly—generously recognized by her classmates;
she did not, however, receive the one accolade she most wanted,
for she lost the election for class poet. Boys outnumbered the
girls in the graduating class and they voted as a solid block for
one of their own sex. Vincent was bitterly disappointed, but
her mother saved the day by suggesting that she write a poem
instead of the conventional commencement essay. When she

recited it at the exercises, the audience applauded as though it were the class poem, and she carried off a ten dollar prize.

Mother, do you know, almost all people love their mothers, but I have never met anybody in my life, I think, who loved his mother as much as I love you. I don't believe there was anybody who did, quite so much, and quite in so many wonderful ways. I was telling somebody yesterday that the reason I am a poet is entirely because you wanted me to be and intended I should be, even from the very first. You brought me up in the tradition of poetry, and everything I did you encouraged. I cannot remember once in my life when you were not interested in what I was working on, or even suggested that I should put it aside for something else.[4]

So Vincent wrote in 1921. But during the summer following high school graduation, 1909, and for several years following, there was little she could do about becoming a professional poet. She was only seventeen years old, much too young to try her wings in Boston or New York, and her family needed her in Camden. She worked as a typist and kept house; she practiced her piano and always continued to write. Fortunately there was *St. Nicholas Magazine,* and the "*St. Nicholas* League," which published contributions from its young readers and gave prizes. "E. Vincent Millay," as she always signed her work, had first appeared under the League banner in 1906 when she was fourteen. After that, she became a constant contributor, and, though her poems were not always accepted for publication, participating in the competitions had one all important effect: it kept her writing. But in 1910, she reached her eighteenth birthday, the age limit set by the League for its participants. She went out in a blaze of glory, winning the top prize—five dollars—for a poem called "Friends," and she wrote to the editors,

Although I shall never write for the League again, I shall not allow myself to become a stranger to it. You have been a great help and a great encouragement to me, and I am sorry to grow up and leave you.[5]

With the prize money she bought "a beautiful copy of Browning, whom I admire so much. . . ." [6]

The pages of *St. Nicholas* were closed to her, and, casting about for another outlet for her poetry, for the first time she began to notice the restrictiveness of her surroundings. Apparently the idea of going to college did not occur to her, nor is this surprising, for college was not yet the usual pattern for a girl's life in 1910. She was not especially interested in boys, though she saw a great many of them, for she and her sisters were attractive and popular, and they regularly received "gentleman callers." She was a member of several girls' clubs, but there was nothing in Camden to remotely approximate "The Potters" of St. Louis. She used to sit for hours at a time looking at the sea, or she took long walks up Mt. Battie or Mt. Megunticook. Up to this time she had been known for her vibrancy and enthusiasm; now she was meditative, even withdrawn. She was still writing, but the realization must have come to her in that summer of 1910 that, just as she herself was slowly climbing up to a new plateau in her own life, so her poetry must change. "Vacation Song," even "Friends" were all very fine for the *St. Nicholas* League, but now they seemed only apprentice attempts. What she wanted to do was write poetry which would "pierce a way into the world's great heart." [7]

That thoughts such as these must have occurred in her meditations is an almost overwhelming certainty, for her next poem, "Renascence," is startlingly different from anything she had previously written. It is cast in the form of a dramatic monologue, perhaps an indication of the Browning influence, but that is about the only influence to be found in it except for one echo of Andrew Marvell. Its preoccupation with eternity is highly reminiscent of Emily Dickinson, the more startling because, at that time, Vincent had read nothing by her great New England predecessor. The deceptively simple opening lines—

> All I could see from where I stood
> Was three long mountains and a wood;

> I turned and looked another way,
> And saw three islands in a bay.

at once evoke the mood of the stark Maine landscape and the emotion of the speaker, Vincent Millay. Bound by the restrictions of her environment, her tone is one of quiet despair which deepens as the poem continues. The claustrophobic imagery when she reaches up her hand and "[screams] to feel it touch the sky" is superb, all the more effective because of its control. Suddenly the poet feels "Infinity" settling over her, and—

> I saw and heard and knew at last
> The How and Why of all things, past,
> And present, and forevermore.

In a mysterious, almost mystic way, she feels the weight of all the world's sorrow and pain:

> A man was starving in Capri;
> He moved his eyes and looked at me;
> I felt his gaze, I heard his moan,
> And knew his hunger as my own.

The burden is too great; she sinks into the ground:

> Into the earth I sank till I
> Full six feet under ground did lie,
> And sank no more,—there is no weight
> Can follow here, however great.

But, although the grave is safe from the world's grief, it is equally remote for its beauty:

> How can I bear it, buried here,
> When overhead the sky grows clear
> And blue again after the storm?

"O God, I cried, give me new birth!" The prayer is heard; the poet springs up from the ground:

> And hailed the earth with such a cry
> As is not heard save from a man
> Who has been dead, and lives again.

Now, fully cognizant of the meaning of evil and death, she knows equally the source of beauty and life:

> O God, I cried, no dark disguise
> Can e'er hereafter hide from me
> Thy radiant identity!

And she knows, too, that man is bound only by his limitations:

> The world stands out on either side
> No wider than the heart is wide;
> Above the world is stretched the sky,—
> No higher than the soul is high. . . .
> But East and West will pinch the heart
> That can not keep them pushed apart;
> And he whose soul is flat—the sky
> Will cave in on him by and by.

"Renascence" would be a remarkable achievement for a poet at the height of his mature powers; for one of eighteen it is almost incredible. But it must be remembered that Vincent Millay had been learning her craft almost from the moment that she could hold a pencil. Her mind, fed by constant reading, had soared far above her chronological age, so that, young as she was, she could handle the most difficult philosophical and theological concepts with amazing ease. In a word, when her moment came, she was ready. How her mother read of *The Lyric Year* contest in a magazine and urged Vincent to send in "Renascence;" how the judges were astounded by it and, though they did not award it first prize or even second or third (much to the disgust of the winners who instantly recognized the poem's calibre and quality); how critics and readers alike praised "Renascence" as the finest work in the entire volume; all this is history. Like Byron, Vincent Millay woke on a November morning in that epic year 1912 to find herself famous, more famous for not having won a prize than if she had. Almost at once she began to hear from other poets; Witter Bynner and Arthur Davidson Ficke, both of whom had appeared in *The Lyric Year*, wrote that they had been "somewhat disheartened" by the volume; "And suddenly we stumbled upon this one ["Renascence"], which really lights up the whole book. It seems to both of us a real vision. . . ." [8]

Like so many others, Bynner and Ficke were convinced that "Miss Edna St. Vincent Millay" must be a pseudonym. Vincent was highly entertained. "Mr. Earle [editor of *The Lyric Year*] acquainted me with your wild surmises," she wrote. "Gentlemen, I must convince you of your error. I simply will not be a brawny male." [9] And she added wittily, "when a woman insists that she is twenty, you must not call her forty-five. That is more than wicked; it is indiscreet." [10]

That publication would bring Vincent much attention might have been anticipated, but "Renascence" was also to open one totally unexpected door.

In the summer of 1912, prior to the publication of *The Lyric Year*, Norma Millay had taken one of the table-waiting jobs at the Whitehall Inn, a more or less traditional occupation for daughters of New England "gentry" at that time. (Twenty years later, such jobs would be avidly sought by college students.) A ball was given for the young ladies, always, and this particular summer Norma insisted that Vincent attend. Entertainment, too, was always furnished by the girls and their guests, and Vincent was persuaded to play some of her own compositions on the piano. Then, at her sister's urging, Vincent recited her soon-to-be-published poem. In the audience of summer visitors at the inn was Caroline Dow, head of the National Training School of the YWCA in New York. Deeply impressed by "Renascence" and by the poet, Miss Dow determined that Vincent must go to college. She made arrangements for her to take some preliminary courses at Barnard during the winter, so that she could apply for a scholarship at Vassar for the following year. Miss Dow's perceptiveness and generosity were never to be forgotten; nine years later Vincent dedicated *Second April* "To my beloved friend, Caroline B. Dow," who, by that time, had become "Aunt Calline."

Vincent Millay arrived in New York in February, 1913. She

enrolled in English 24 at Barnard; if there were other courses, her letters do not mention them, and this is not especially surprising. English 24 was taught by William Tenney Brewster (one of the professorial greats), as a writing course, and writing was her principle interest. There were many distractions. Everyone wanted to meet her; the Poetry Society gave a luncheon in her honor at which Witter Bynner read "Renascence" because the poet was overcome by an unusual case of stage fright and could not do so herself. Sara Teasdale invited her to tea; Jessie Rittenhouse held a "Literary Evening," at which the Edwin Markhams and Anna Hempstead Branch were among the guests. Her letters to her family reveal her excitement over that occasion, and also an amusing insight into her reactions towards one of the several fringe benefits of success. There was a young artist "that Miss Branch is very anxious to fall in love with me and me with him," she wrote humorously. "She doesn't suspect I know it. But you should hear her talk about him to me. I can't help wondering if she says the same kind of things about me to him." [11] The artist was only one of a number of men whom Vincent met that winter and who were greatly attracted to her; in fact, over the next ten years, until she fell in love with Eugen Boissevain and married him, so many men were linked romantically with Vincent Millay that Edmund Wilson (himself a leading contender) once remarked that they should form an alumni association! But Vincent was not about even to consider marriage in 1913. She had made up her mind to go to Vassar, and, tempting as staying in New York might be, she would not alter her decision. She did sell two poems—"Journey" and "O world, I cannot hold thee close enough"—to *Forum*; "Louis Untermeyer and Sara Teasdale are crazy about them both," she wrote ecstatically to her mother, enclosing a check for $25.00 with the request,

Promise me, please, that with some of this you'll do something to make something easier for yourself. Shoes, dear,—or have your glasses fixed if they're not just right. Please, please, do something

like that. And I'd like it so much if each one of you would get some
little tiny silly thing that she could always keep. But that's just a
whim; the other isn't.[12]

She returned to Camden in June to study for the entrance
examinations for Vassar; they were as difficult as she had anticipated, but, to her intense relief, she passed them successfully,
and arrived in Poughkeepsie in September, 1913.

She was twenty-one, four years older than the other freshmen,
and far beyond them intellectually. Her family background had
accustomed her to taking responsibility, and, though she had
lived under "Aunt Calline's" watchful eye, she nevertheless had
enjoyed considerable freedom in New York. And she was a
recognized, published poet, who had received considerable acclaim. That she wanted to go to college at all indicates both
courage and perseverance on her part, for this was not the day of
"continuing" or "adult" education. But nothing had prepared
her for the restrictiveness of life on a woman's college campus in
1913. Though accustomed to discipline, all her life she had
usually been permitted to follow her impulses as long as she did
not actually break the rules or act discourteously. In Camden
she had frequently gone for a walk alone on a moonlight night;
when she did the same thing at Vassar the head warden was
appalled. Vincent simply could not understand such a reaction.
Had no one there ever heard of a girl's wanting to take a walk
alone at night? Her irritation was the greater, perhaps, because
it seemed to her that the head warden and her associates were
assuming that she must be doing it for some ulterior reason,
whereas for Vincent the moon, the night, and walking were
reason enough.

Then, there was the matter of class attendance. Naturally she
continued to write poetry, and, if inspiration struck during a
time when she was supposed to be in the classroom, the poem
came first. A procedure not calculated to win friends and influence professors! The story is told of how she once sent a note
to a professor, excusing herself from his class because of illness;

later that day he met her on campus and commented on her quick recovery. To which Vincent replied with perfect honesty, "I was giving birth to a poem." [13] Yet her essays were invariably brilliant, and her examinations were the best in the class. Her phenomenal memory stood her in good stead, and she was capable of an intensive concentration which made it possible for her to absorb in a few hours what it might take the average student twice as long to acquire.

She was fortunate, too, in that Henry Noble MacCracken was president of Vassar during her four years there. She spent a great deal of time in his office listening to his remonstrances, making good use of the extra handkerchiefs which he kept in his desk drawer for students during such interviews. Once she took two away with her and washed and ironed them beautifully herself before returning them. Finally Dr. MacCracken told her quietly that he "knew all about poets at colleges," and that he did not want "a banished Shelley on his doorstep." Do what she would, he would *not* expel her. To which Vincent replied haughtily, "On those terms, I think I can continue to live in this hell hole." [14] It was the most sensible thing Dr. Mac-Cracken could have done. Deprived of the assurance that sensational consequences would attend her breaking the rules, she began to see the advantages of the "pink-and-gray college" [15] she had hated so, and by May of her freshman year she was writing to her mother, "I'm crazy about college and everything." [16]

"Everything" comprised a great deal. The academic curriculum was stiff and demanding. Vincent fulfilled all requirements in English literature, history, mathematics, science, and philosophy, and then worked intensively in English literature, including Old English and Chaucer. She had a flair for languages, so she elected courses in Latin, Greek, French, German, Italian and Spanish literature. Naturally she took all the advanced composition courses. As a result of these, or perhaps simply because of her own interest in the theatre, she quickly became involved in college dramatics and wrote several plays: *The Princess Marries the Page, The Wall of Dominoes,* and *Two Slat-*

terns and a King. She was the best actress on campus, and she seriously began to consider a theatrical career—an ambition which received a special impetus when she met the actress Edith Wynne Mathison, on one of the several occasions when she and her playwright husband, Charles Rann Kennedy, visited Vassar. The Kennedys more or less adopted Vincent, and helped her in every possible way during her first year in New York after graduation.

Vassar also offered great opportunities for a student talented in musical composition. Each class had its own collection of original songs for every occasion—opening day of classes, freshman initiation, sophomore tree planting, Founders Day, senior class day, plus songs for informal "class sings." Rivalry between the four classes was intense, and the annual song contest held on Founders Day was one of the most important events of the year. Vincent won the prize for her class in 1916; in 1917, the year she graduated, she wrote the lyrics and composed the music to the baccalaureate hymn. It is a most effective work, both musically and verbally; the fourth verse especially,

> Since we are dust, how shall we not betray Thee?
> Still blows about the world the ancient wind—
> Not yet for lives untried and tearless would we pray Thee:
> Lord let us suffer that we may grow kind!

is prophetic, in a sense, of Vincent Millay's future.

It must be noted, too, that she was in a woman's college at the time when "woman's rights" were being most fiercely agitated, especially the right to vote. Dr. MacCracken was squarely and unequivocally on the side of women in the campaign, and was not at all displeased when the students became involved in that issue. To Vassar, in 1915, came Inez Millholland, returning to visit her alma mater as one of the leaders of the suffrage movement; Vincent was in the audience on the evening of her lecture, and this occasion may have marked the beginning of her own personal commitment to the advancement of women. (Also in the audience was Eugen Boissevain, who, at that time, was married to Inez Millholland, and who was ultimately to play a major role in Vincent's life.) In every way her years at Vassar were stimulating and exciting, and it must be admitted that Vincent herself was a considerable source of both the excitement and stimulation.

Even her graduation precipitated a major crisis. She had been campused for an infraction of the rules, then—quite heedlessly, as she later admitted—she had broken campus. Suspension was the penalty; she would receive her diploma, but she would not be permitted to graduate with her class. Her friends—who numbered almost the entire student body—rallied behind her; they wrote letters of protest and circulated petitions, which they presented to Dr. MacCracken. That gentleman found himself in a quandary; he had the power of veto over all decisions, and he had promised himself that he would never use it. After lengthy consideration, however, he did use it, for the first and last time in his presidency, because—as he said later—"there were few students who had done more for their college than this young poet." [17] Vincent marched in the commencement procession of June, 1917, then took the next train to New York to look for an acting job.

She was unsuccessful—June, generally, is not a good time to find a part in a play—but she was not especially concerned. She decided to return to Camden for the summer; she was working on her first book, and writing, she felt, could be done anywhere. Late in August the Kennedys invited her to visit them in Connecticut, and to return with them to New York in mid-September. Poetry readings, arranged through Mrs. Kennedy's influence, and a few sales of poems to magazines brought in some money; then, in December, *"Renascence" and Other Poems* was published and was a resounding success. Now she could afford an apartment of her own; Norma came to New York to be with her, and the two sisters took an apartment in Greenwich Village.

The Greenwich Village of pre-World War I was a far cry from that of the 1960's. Everett Shinn, the celebrated artist, who maintained his studio on a corner of Washington Square until his death in 1953, described the Village enthusiastically and graphically as:

. . . an exciting place where *most* of the people were on their way up the ladder. Oh, there were the hangers-on, of course—there always are. People who think that artiness is art, and phoniness is creativity. But the ones I knew were young and very serious about their work—never about themselves!—or they'd never have made the grade. We lived in the Village because it was cheap. Arthur Hopkins and I shared an apartment, and we often put on plays. Ben Ali Hagen did the sets, and sometimes we gave the Washington Square and Provincetown crowd a run for their money! We came to New York because it offered opportunities that we couldn't find at home. Of course we enjoyed ourselves! We were doing what we most wanted to do, and that's the only real happiness there is. I'll admit we weren't exactly conventional. The girls bobbed their hair and smoked cigarettes; the WCTU heartily disapproved of us, and there was a certain amount of what the clergy called "free love." But the difference between the Village then and now—and the important thing to remember—is that we didn't finally make it as poets or artists or actors or playwrights *because* we were *unconventional*. It was because we had talent, and we worked. We knew we had to, if our success was to be worth a damn! And we had ideals, too, believe it or not. We wanted to do something with our gifts to add to the beauty of the world. There was a war going on in Europe—long before *you* were born—none of us knew when America would get into it, or when we might be called, and beauty seemed in danger of vanishing. We wanted to save it, while we still had time.[18]

In the Village, Vincent Millay quickly found her unique place. At twenty-five she was a recognized poet—but she wanted more. She wanted greatness. Like all poets she hoped for immortality through her work, but she was not an Emily Dickinson, willing to write a "letter to the world," and to live in hope of one day being discovered. In an almost arrogant, yet confident poem, "The Poet and His Book," she issued commands:

Stranger, pause and look;
        From the dust of ages
Lift this little book,
        Turn the tattered pages,
Read me, do not let me die!
        Search the fading letters, finding
        Steadfast in the broken binding
All that once was I!

For she believed that poetry was inextricably woven into the fabric of life; that the poet's words can bring relevance and insight to every human situation:

Women at your toil,
        Women at your leisure
Till the kettle boil,
        Snatch of me your pleasure,
Where the broom-straw marks the leaf;
        Women quiet with your weeping
        Lest you wake a workman sleeping,
Mix me with your grief!

For her, poetry was the supreme fact of her own existence, and nothing could be allowed to stand in its way. In one of her last, and most dramatic sonnets, she was to give her reason for this deep sense of dedication and responsibility to her art:

If I die solvent—die, that is to say,
In full possession of my critical mind,
Not having cast, to keep the wolves at bay
In this dark wood—till all be flung behind—
Wit, courage, honour, pride, oblivion
Of the red eyeball and the yellow tooth;
Nor sweat nor howl nor break into a run
When loping Death's upon me in hot sooth;
'Twill be that in my honoured hands I bear
What's under no condition to be spilled
Till my blood spills and hardens in the air:
An earthen grail, a humble vessel filled
To its low brim with water from that brink
Where Shakespeare, Keats, and Chaucer
                                learned to drink.

Though she never said it in so many words, she, too—either intuitively or by direct influence through her early reading of the great Victorians—knew the meaning of Carlyle's concept of the *vates*, the poet-prophet, and of Tennyson's ideal of the poet as one who "with his word" shook the world.

It was her dedication to poetry that was the principal barrier to her establishing at this time any enduring relationship with any man. *Post hoc* Freudian analysis has found in many of her poems concerning the transiency of love, and in her celebrated admission, "I am most faithless when I most am true," an unconscious revelation of a deep fear of love, resulting from her parents' divorce. That she was afraid is possible, but it is equally possible that the truth of the matter is to be found in another poetic admission: "After the feet of beauty fly my own." That men surrounded her is certainly true, but the surprising thing is that none of them seemed excessively jealous of the others; as Edmund Wilson wrote in his memoir of her, ". . . the other thing was always there . . . Her poetry, you soon found out, was her real overmastering passion." [19] Wilson was one of the men who proposed to her; Floyd Dell, who gave her a role in his *The Angel Intrudes* when it was produced by the Provincetown Players in December, 1917, was another. Certainly she loved them both, in different ways and for different reasons, as she also loved Arthur Davidson Ficke, to whom she wrote one of the most beautiful love letters ever penned.

But she knew herself well. As a poet, she was a highly emotional person, capable both of deep affection and passionate response; she was also practical and sensible enough to recognize that even the most passionate and genuine love, could be transient:

> After all, my erstwhile dear,
> My no longer cherished,
> Need we say it was not love,
> Just because it perished?

Marriage, however, meant lifelong commitment. She could not write to a husband,

I know I am but summer to your heart,
And not the full four seasons of the year;

and, at this juncture, a husband could not write otherwise of her.

Nevertheless, the men who loved her remained her friends; and her loyalty to them continued as long as she lived. When Floyd Dell, as an editor of *Masses* magazine, was arrested and tried for sedition in April, 1918, because *Masses* had strongly opposed America's entry into World War I, she went to the courtroom to stand by him; she did so again, in September of that same year, when a second trial became necessary because the first ended in a hung jury. But she would not marry him, or anyone else, to whom she could not be—and who could not be to her—"the full four seasons of the year."

It was perhaps out of these romances which conflicted sharply with her dedication to poetry that the wryly humorous, bittersweet verses published in 1920 under the title *A Few Figs from Thistles* was born. The book made a sensation; it combined with *The Harp-Weaver* and twenty sonnets published in Reedy's *Mirror* to win for Vincent the Pulitzer Prize for Poetry, the first woman ever so honored. *A Few Figs from Thistles* certainly captured the spirit of the age, which was restless, irreverent often to the point of insolence, and, to use a favorite contemporary idiom, "cool." Readers, especially the teenage and college groups, recognized immediately that Vincent Millay had given voice to their own defiance, their own protest against established discipline, their avidity to flout conventional mores and manners and to live as they pleased. Such verses as,

My candle burns at both the ends;
It will not last the night;
But ah, my foes, and oh, my friends,
It gives a lovely light!

and,

Safe upon the rock the ugly houses stand:
Come and see my shining palace built upon the sand!

were perfectly in exact accord with the hedonism that swept the country in the post-World-War-I years—the Jazz Age, speakeasies, and all the other components of an era trying to hide its disillusion with the "war to end all wars" under a mask of frenzied gaiety. Vincent Millay voiced the spirit of the Twenties in such a poem as "Thursday"—

> And if I loved you Wednesday,
>   Well, what is that to you?
> I do not love you Thursday—
>   So much is true.
>
> And why you come complaining
>   Is more than I can see.
> I loved you Wednesday,—yes—but what
>   Is that to me?

In "The Penitent," she dared to say that she was not especially sorry—

> . . . "One thing there's no getting by—
> I've been a wicked girl," said I;
> "But if I can't be sorry, why,
>   I might as well be glad!"

And she even stated that, *of course,* her love for the man of the moment will not last:

> I shall forget you presently, my dear,
> So make the most of this, your little day.

But the poems in A *Few Figs from Thistles* did not altogether mask the inner spirit of Vincent Millay. In "To the Not Impossible Him"—one of the most charming in the volume— she betrays her own restless, questing nature, and a genuine weariness with the importunings of those who cannot understand what she is really searching for—an unfair weariness, since she does not altogether know herself what she wants. Even more revealing is a poem written about this time, but not included among the "Figs:"

Thanks be to God the world is wide,
    And I am going far from home,
For I forgot in Camelot
    The man I loved in Rome,

And I forgot in Kensington
    The man I loved in Kew;
And there must be a place for me
    To think no more of you.[20]

At first glance, this poem seems another charming trifle, but here is an excellent example of art concealing artfulness. Camelot is associated with the legendary King Arthur; Kensington with Peter Pan. Both may be said, then, to symbolize an imaginary world, to which the poet retreats from actuality to find some kind of healing oblivion. One might ask why a successful poet whose work was in great demand, and a short story writer who published in *Vanity Fair* under the pseudonym of "Nancy Boyd," whose anti-war play *Aria Da Capo* had been triumphantly produced by the Provincetown Players, should feel a need for either Camelot or Kensington. Apparently she did, however, for she wrote to her mother in December, 1920,

. . . I have decided that the thing for me to do is to have a change—change of everything—so I am going to travel . . . my work, more than anything else, my poetry, I mean, needs fresh grass to feed on. I am becoming sterile here; I have known it would be, and I see it approaching if I stay here.[21]

Then, the revealing addition, "Also, New York is getting too congested for me,—too many people; I get no time to work." [22]

She had also suffered a series of illnesses in the autumn of 1920, and admitted to her mother that she had been through "another small nervous breakdown." The feeling that she had reached a frustrating barrier is apparent in *Second April*, which she was preparing for publication at that time. Many of the poems in that volume reveal her longing to be free of the city:

Searching my heart for its true sorrow,
  This is the thing I find to be:
That I am weary of words and people,
  Sick of the city, wanting the sea;

"The Death of Autumn," with its poignant last lines,

. . . . I know that Beauty must ail and die,
And will be born again,—but ah, to see
Beauty stiffened, staring up at the sky!
Oh Autumn! Autumn!—What is the Spring to me?

indicates that the faith of "Renascence" is still with her, but
the poet is now "clinging heaven by the hems." And conflict of
love and poetry is to be found in the earnest plea,

Into the golden Vessel of great song
Let us pour all our passion;

. . . and in the question,

Cherish you then the hope I shall forget
At length, my lord, Pieria?—put away
For your so passing sake, this mouth of clay,
These mortal bones against my body set
For all the puny fever and frail sweat
Of human love,—renounce for these, I say,
The Singing Mountain's memory, and betray
The silent lyre that hangs upon me yet?

Yet her own "golden Vessel" had been filled to the brim, and
her lyre was almost silent. The fear of being unable to write
assailed her. Clearly she needed to get away for a time from
the both-ends candle-burning life, and also the confusion
wrought by adulation that might, if permitted, keep her from
the self-knowledge that she needed in order to be the poet it
was in her to be. Like others before her, she was experiencing
the need for solitude in which to create.

So, like many other Americans in the Twenties, she went to
Paris. She arrived in January, 1921, as "foreign correspondent"
for *Vanity Fair*; the magazine would pay for two articles a

month, one under her own name, the other by "Nancy Boyd."
Just as she had been discovered by the Village four years earlier,
so she was in Paris by the American artists, poets, novelists and
musicians who had also taken up residence in the city by the
Seine. She met F. Scott Fitzgerald, Edgar Lee Masters, Stephen
and William Rose Benet, and Deems Taylor. She visited the
museums and went to the night clubs, where she astonished all
beholders with her accomplished dancing. That September she
went to Normandy, then to Rome, then on a horseback trip
through Albania and the area that had been Montenegro. She
spent part of the winter in Vienna, which she hated; February,
1922, found her in Budapest. Deliberately she had written no
poetry for a year. She began a novel, which she would ultimately
abandon, but at least, now, she *wanted* to write again.

In April she returned to Paris, where her mother joined her,
not a moment too soon. Vincent was suffering from gastroen-
teritus (she said later that she "came within an ace of having
peritonitis"),[23] brought on by improper food and the general
neglect of her health. Paris was much too hectic; to find some
peace and quiet, her mother took her to England, where they
leased a cottage in Dorset for the summer and autumn, and
here Vincent began to work at her poetry again. By December,
she had recovered sufficiently to take her mother to the South
of France for a few weeks; then they sailed for home in January, 1923.

But Vincent was still far from completely well. She could not
finish her novel, and readying another volume of poems for
publication was proving almost a Herculean task. Fortune,
however, once again played into her hands; at the home of
friends, she met Eugen Boissevain. Actually she had met him
casually several years earlier, but the occasion had not been
especially memorable. This meeting, however, was different indeed. On May 30, she wrote to her mother,

Darling, do you remember meeting Eugen Boissevain one day in
Waverly Place?—it was only for a moment, and possibly you don't

remember. But anyway, you will like him very much when you do know him, which will be soon. And it is important that you should like him,—because I love him very much & am going to marry him.[24]

"Some men are born to be husbands of prima donnas," John Hall Wheelock has remarked,[25] and Eugen Boissevain was one of that highly unusual breed. He was born in Amsterdam, where his father was editor of Holland's leading newspaper; his mother was Irish, the daughter of the Provost of Trinity College, Dublin. He was a handsome, substantial, wealthy widower, whose first marriage to Inez Millholland had been extremely happy. He was twelve years older than Vincent, and there was no question about his willingness for her to continue in her profession, for he was deeply in love with her. "Anyone can buy and sell coffee," he said, referring to his own highly successful import business, "but anyone cannot write poetry." [26]

Convinced of Vincent's importance to the world as a poet, this man was perfectly willing to let his own work and even himself take second place, since this seemed to provide for her the ambience that she needed. When her work required solitude and quiet, he was her shield against intrusion; when she wanted company, he was a delighted, and therefore delightful, companion. Even more important, his mind was sufficiently brilliant and perceptive—and sympathetic—to complement hers. "Vincent and I may get into an interesting discussion at six in the morning, and at noon we are still not dressed, still talking, tremendously excited by ideas," he remarked shortly after their marriage. "We read books together; we tramp about; she talks over a new poem with me. . . ." [27] In one moving statement, he summed up his own *raison d'être*: "Any day I may have an hour of extraordinary beauty." [28] He refused to be angered when outsiders, who could not understand their unique relationship, referred to him as "Mr. Edna St. Vincent Millay." In fact, he met such allegations with genuine laughter. No one who knew him could doubt that Eugen Boissevain was a remarkable person in his own right, and Vincent loved and respected him first and foremost for that reason.

They were married on the morning of July 18, 1923, and, indicative of Eugen's care for her, that same afternoon, she entered a New York hospital to prepare for extensive surgery to correct the condition which had caused her severe illness in Europe, and from which she had suffered acutely ever since. Her new book, "The Harp Weaver" and Other Poems was ready to go to press, but the operation left her so very weak that Eugen decreed she could do no work whatever. She willingly did not try, and abided by his decision. Arthur Davidson Ficke, her old friend, corrected the proofs, and the book was successfully published late that autumn. "The Ballad of the Harp Weaver," which she wrote in part as a tribute to her mother, is probably her best known and loved poem, but there are others in the collection which must be numbered among her most distinguished works. For example, "Feast"—evocative of Emily Dickinson, but equally, uniquely Millay:

> I drank at every vine.
>   The last was like the first.
> I came upon no wine
>   So wonderful as thirst.

"The Spring and the Fall" centers on a familiar theme, the transiency of love, but the lines:

> He laughed at all I dared to praise,
> And broke my heart, in little ways.

and the final stanza:

> Year be springing or year be falling,
> The bark will drip and the birds be calling.
> There's much that's fine to see and hear
> In the spring of a year, in the fall of a year.
> 'Tis not love's going hurts my days,
> But that it went in little ways.

indicate an insight and maturity not to be found in her earlier poetry. The brittle-bright tone of *Figs* and the rather self-contemplating bitterness of *Second April* (which called forth Amy Lowell's criticism) are absent. Also, some of her finest sonnets are in *"The Harp Weaver"* volume, a form which she especially loved and insisted upon bringing to her own standard of perfection despite the furore over the "new poetry," or the "stream of consciousness" approach used by T. S. Eliot in "The Wasteland," which had been published in 1922.

Vincent did not fully recover from her surgical ordeal until the beginning of 1924. The moment she felt strong enough, she embarked on her first reading tour; she was determined to pay off certain debts she had contracted before her marriage, and to help her mother financially without Eugen's assistance. She accomplished both, but at great sacrifice to her health and she returned to New York exhausted. This time, fortunately, she could return to Eugen. He took her on a cruise to the Orient and then around the world, making it possible for her to rest for almost a year. When they returned, they decided definitely that they did not want to live in New York any longer—it was too hectic and crowded, and Vincent wanted a garden. So, in the spring of 1925, Eugen bought a farm at Austerlitz, New York, which they called "Steepletop." On seven hundred acres on the Berkshire slopes, they were to make their home for the rest of their lives.

At Steepletop, and also on Ragged Island, which they bought in 1933 so that Vincent could occasionally have the solitude by the sea that she so loved, the Boissevains could lead the kind of life that they both enjoyed. There was a special "Poetry Room" for Vincent's collection of poetry in many different languages; on the wall, alongside portraits of Robinson Jeffers and Shelley, was a large sign—"Silence." There was no telephone. During the winter, Eugen walked into Austerlitz, three miles away, on snowshoes for mail and provisions. Steepletop was run as a working farm and there was considerable activity, so a small cottage a little distant from the main house was fitted out as a private retreat for Vincent when she wanted to work undisturbed. One thing noted by all visitors was the quantity of scratch pads and pencils in every room, for the poet who never knew when inspiration would strike. Visitors were always welcome at Steepletop, but preferably by appointment. Eugen knew very well how quickly Vincent could become exhausted by entertaining friends, and equally well how she could tie herself into knots of inner resentment at the need to "socialize" when she had planned to work—

> . . . I avoid the looming visitor,
> Flee him adroitly around corners,
> Hating him, wishing him well;
> Lest if he confront me I be forced to say what is
> in no wise true:
> That he is welcome; that I am unoccupied;
> And forced to sit while the potted roses wilt in the
> crate or the sonnet cools.

Eugen became a protector against intruders who wanted to see Edna St. Vincent Millay merely in order to be able to say that they had seen her. And he could always accomplish this very delicate manoeuvre in a manner that did not antagonize the intruders against himself or the poet.

The years between 1925 and 1943 were the most productive of Vincent Millay's career. 1926 was taken up with writing a libretto for Deems Taylor's opera *The King's Henchman*, the first American opera to be given a premiere at the Metropolitan in twelve years. On opening night, February 17, 1927, there was a twenty minute ovation during which composer and librettist were repeatedly called on stage. Vincent's greatest joy was that her mother could be present to see her triumph, as well as the knowledge that her work had silenced once and for all the contention that opera in English was impossible. In 1928, she published *The Buck in the Snow*, and in 1929 *Poems Selected For Young People*. *Fatal Interview*, judged the finest sonnet sequence of the twentieth century, appeared in 1931; *Wine From These Grapes* in 1934; *Conversation At Midnight* (the original manuscript of which was destroyed by fire in a Florida hotel where she and Eugen were spending the winter, and had to be rewritten from memory) in 1937; and *Huntsman, What Quarry?*

in 1938. In collaboration with George Dillon she translated Charles Baudelaire's *Les Fleurs du Mal,* which was published in 1936. Her poetry-reading tours became annual events, and in the winter of 1932–33, she gave a weekly series over Radio Station WJZ which, much to the astonishment of the management, achieved unequivocal success.

She was also periodically involved in causes. She was one of several writers to protest the execution of Sacco and Vanzetti, and she presented her poem "Justice Denied in Massachusetts" for the first time at a mass vigil meeting in Boston on the night of August 22, 1927. She, along with John Dos Passos, was arrested and taken to the police station for participating in a protest march; after Eugen appeared with her bail money, she obtained an audience with Governor Fuller and made a strong plea for clemency. Vincent felt sincerely that the guilt of Sacco and Vanzetti for the murder of two men in South Braintree had not been proved beyond all shadow of a doubt; indeed, she maintained that the alleged anarchistic beliefs of the two men had been the major factor in their conviction. When clemency was denied, it seemed to her that the concept of equal justice for all had received a leveling blow. Her poem, especially the bitter last lines, echoes the sentiment of the times:

> Let us sit here, sit still,
> Here in the sitting-room until we dic;
> At the step of Death on the walk, rise and go;
> Leaving to our children's children this beautiful
> > doorway,
> And this elm,
> And a blighted earth to till
> With a broken hoe.

Certainly this episode made an indelible impression on her; she saw all too clearly the ugly mass hysteria engendered by the Sacco-Vanzetti case, and was sickened by it. No longer was she so willing to believe in man's inherent nobility; in "My Spirit, Sore from Marching," she wrote with unaccustomed bitterness:

> Draw from the shapeless moment
> Such pattern as you can;

And cleave henceforth to Beauty;
Expect no more from man.

The depression she was suffering was accentuated by recurrent
bouts of illness; as she wrote Arthur Davidson Ficke, describing
an influenza siege in the autumn of 1930,

It's not true that life is one damn thing after another—it's one
damn thing over & over—there's the rub—first you get sick—then
you get sicker—then you get not quite so sick—then you get hardly
sick at all—then you get a little sicker—then you get a lot sicker—
then you get not quite so sick—oh, hell! [29]

Even spending the winters abroad or in Florida, with Eugen's
devoted care, seemed to do little but help her to recover from
one attack in time to succumb to the next. In 1936 she was in a
terrible automobile accident, in which her right arm, shoulder,
and several nerves in her back were injured; the full effect of
the accident did not become apparent immediately, with the
result that she struggled for three years against constantly increasing pain until, finally, in 1939, she suffered a complete collapse.

But necessity drove her back to her desk. The coming of
World War II wiped out the Boissevain interests in the Dutch
East Indies, and almost overnight Eugen's fortune was gone.
Steepletop had to be mortgaged, and Vincent had to support
them both. Then, in 1940, Hitler's armies overran Holland. Vincent was one of the vocal minority, amidst the general apathy,
who recognized Hitler's battle plan—first, absorb Europe, then,
with the help of Japan, attack America. The Luftwaffe had already demonstrated how entire countries could be "softened
up" by repeated bombing prior to the actual invasion, and
America's military defenses were not prepared to confront
either trans-oceanic planes or aircraft carrier based Messer-
schmidts. Nor were her coastlines protected against submarines,
which the Nazis were known to possess in quantity.

No one was more pacifist by nature than Vincent Millay. Yet, as the days wore on, she became more and more convinced that unless America armed herself against all possible contingencies, she could not survive. Once before Vincent had used her poetry for social comment during the Sacco-Vanzetti case; now even less would her conscience let her rest. The result of her conviction and—surely New England!—evangelical zeal was *Make Bright The Arrows*, poems written exclusively as propaganda, beginning with the clarion command:

> Make bright the arrows,
>   O peaceful and wise!
> Gather the shields
>   Against surprise.

"I know quite well there are thousands of people, true lovers of poetry . . . who will, no matter what I write in the future, never forgive me for writing this book," [30] she wrote to Charlotte Babcock Sills, her former roommate at Vassar. Mrs. Sills, the mother of three draft-age sons, had been greatly dismayed by *Make Bright The Arrows*, and had written to tell Vincent that if *she* had children, she would think differently—she would not be so eager to plunge America into war. Vincent replied that the entire purpose of the book had been to mobilize America's strength so that war might be avoided, and that her having had sons would *not* make her think differently. "I have one thing to give in the service of my country—my reputation as a poet," she wrote.

Have you the slightest conception of what this reputation means to me, who have been building it carefully for more than twenty years, taking a long time, months, sometimes as long as several years before permitting a poem to be published, because I felt that one line of it, one syllable, was not as close to perfection as I might make it? [31]

She knew that *Make Bright The Arrows* was bad, and, as she had predicted, its publication did her considerable damage. Critics who had been captured by "The Waste Land" had, seemingly, been lying in wait for Edna St. Vincent Millay to do inferior work; now they pounced in a pack. But she would not be deflected. "I have enlisted for the duration," [32] she said, and she meant it.

Her next major work was a dramatic narrative commemorating one of the most terrible outrages of World War II, the total destruction of Lidice, a small Czechoslovakian village, in reprisal for the death of Reinhardt Heydrich, Nazi administrator for that region. To the present generation, to whom the appalling events of World War II seem as remote as the Middle Ages and even more unbelievable, Millay's *The Murder of Lidice* may seem a literary curiosity. But those who heard it broadcast on October 19, 1942, with Paul Muni, Alexander Woolcott, and Clifton Fadiman taking the various parts, felt the impact of this really fine work in its own time. It would be difficult to overestimate its influence in arousing American determination to resist and finally to conquer the perpetrators of this and similar atrocities. Vincent Millay continued to serve her country in the only way she could; on June 6, 1944, when the entire world waited agonizingly for word from the Normandy beaches, her "Poem and Prayer for an Invading Army" was read over NBC by the actor Ronald Coleman. In simple, profoundly moving language, the poet called to all America.

> They must not go alone
> Into that burned building!—which today
> is all of Europe.
>   Say
> that you go with them, spirit, and heart, and mind!
> Although the body
> too old to fight a young man's war or wounded
> too deeply under the healed and whitened scar
> of earlier battles, must remain behind.

Regrettably, "Poem and Prayer for an Invading Army" has shared the same opprobrium as *Make Bright The Arrows*. "A poet's first obligation is to his craft," the critical dictum ran, so, in writing this kind of poetry, Vincent Millay was considered to have lowered herself as an artist. Her own answer to that censure was delayed until her posthumous collection, *Mine The Harvest*, was published, which contained one of her finest sonnets:

> And if I die, because that part of me
> Which part alone of me had chance to live,
> Chose to be honour's threshing-floor, a sieve
> Where right through wrong might make its way, and be;
> If from all taint of indignation, free
> Must be my art, and thereby fugitive
> From all that threatens it—why—let me give
> To moles my dubious immortality.
> For, should I cancel by one passionate screed
> All that in chase reflection I have writ,
> So that again not ever in bright need
> A man shall want my verse and reach for it,
> I and my verses will be dead indeed,—
> That which we died to champion, hurt no whit.

With clarity and integrity she had made her decision; having made it, the need for self-justification to blind imperceptiveness, which chose to ignore her plainly stated reasons for her action, must have been infuriating.

That she should suffer physically, as well as spiritually and intellectually, was inevitable. In the summer of 1944, she again suffered a breakdown and spent months in the hospital. For two years, she was unable to write. Her one comfort, apart from Eugen, was that she could still memorize poetry, and, by doing this, gradually she was able to put pencil to paper again. By 1947, she was able to write to her publishers that she was preparing a new volume. She refused to be hurried; she worked steadily and quietly, grateful that the joy of work had returned. It seemed as though once again her own world would be, as nearly as possible, as it had been before the devastation of war. Then, quite suddenly, on August 30, 1949, Eugen died.

She collapsed completely. A long period in the hospital followed; when she recovered, she insisted upon returning to Steepletop alone. Somehow she struggled through the winter,

and, even more difficult, through the spring without her husband. Gradually her natural resilience and independence re-
asserted themselves, and she took hold at Steepletop as Eugen
would have wished. By August, 1950, she could write to her
editor, ". . . it is so wonderful to be writing again! My only
hope, just now. . . ." [33] In one of her notebooks, on an autumn day when the Berkshires were aflame in all their glory, she
wrote the poignant, resolute lines:

> I will control myself, or go inside.
> I will not flaw perfection with my grief.
> Handsome, this day: no matter who has died.[34]

The poem was never to be finished. At dawn, on the nineteenth of October, she was on her way up to bed, having stayed
awake all night to read the proofs of a new translation of the
Aeneid. Evidently a sudden rush of weakness overcame her, for,
late that afternoon, when the handyman opened the door, he
found her lying at the foot of the stairs.

"The problem about Vincent Millay," Marianne Moore has
said, "is that she was popular for all the wrong reasons." [35] This
perceptive comment by a great poet about one of her contemporaries provides an excellent starting point for any evaluation
of Millay's achievement. With its usual proclivity for praising its
own thoughts and ideas in print, a particular reading public—
that of the Twenties and early Thirties—seized on Vincent's
early poetry and perhaps gave it more praise than it deserved.
But this same public, grown older and wiser, refused to accord
the poet the same privilege, and became confused and resentful
when she wrote more seriously. The war poetry seemed a betrayal of an image they had cherished, and her last and really
finest volume was virtually ignored. *A Few Figs From Thistles*
became a kind of mariner's albatross; like Swinburne, who was
never permitted to forget that he had once written "Dolores,"
so her bright quatrains were quoted, anthologized, and perpetu-
ated, until today almost everyone can quote "My candle burns"
ad infinitum, while the remarkable love sonnets of *Fatal Interview* and other poems equally as fine remain unknown.

Her posthumous collection, Mine The Harvest, over which she worked long and carefully, has been published so recently (1954) that it makes a proper perspective difficult. But this may be just as well. Cold objectivity was not one of Vincent Millay's salient characteristics; she was emotional and subjective, and her poetry is far too personal to yield much to purely objective appraisal:

> Cruel of heart, lay down my song.
> Your reading eyes have done me wrong.
> Not for you was the pen bitten,
> And the mind wrung, and the song written.

This quatrain addressed "To Those Without Pity" was published in 1928. In Mine The Harvest, twenty-six years later, she again stated her criticism of the critics in no uncertain terms:

> It is the fashion now to wave aside
> As tedious, obvious, vacuous, trivial, trite,
> All things which do not tickle, tease, excite
> To some subversion, or in verbiage hide
> Intent, or mock, or with hot sauce provide
> A dish to prick the thickened appetite;
> Straightforwardness is wrong, evasions right;
> It is correct, de rigeur to deride.

For Vincent Millay believed that poetry must be honest, and intelligible—she described the writing of a sonnet by saying, "I will put Chaos into fourteen lines/and keep him there." In another poem, she says that a poet must have powers "such as must qualify a god," to create:

> . . . not from dream,
> No, not from aspiration, not from hope,
> But out of art and wisdom. . . .

The word art refers to technical skill, what she called "the skill of the artisan, which every writer who has written for many years, at length acquires." [36] But the word may also be interpreted as that selective, utterly truthful view of reality which a poet achieves by putting "Chaos into fourteen lines"—by successfully verbalizing the inexpressible aspiration, hope, or dream. Greatness in poetry does not consist in putting reality on paper, but, through the power of language, giving the impression of reality—reality heightened and deepened, and all the more true, even though, paradoxically, the poetic reality is not actually "real." Vincent Millay possessed this gift in the highest degree, and achieved her finest poems by first writing down the inspiration the moment it came, and then by chipping away each superfluous word or unharmonious sound. Sometimes she would work for years over a poem, until it satisfied her highest standards.

And, once the poem was as perfect as she could make it, she would allow no changes:

Any changes which might profitably be made in any of my poems, were either made by me, before I permitted them to be published, or must be made, if made at all, someday by me. Only I, who know what I mean to say, and how I want to say it, am competent to deal with such matters. Many of my poems, of course, are greatly reduced in stature from the majesty which I had hoped they might achieve, because I was unable, as one too often is, to make the poem rise up to my conception of it. However, the faults as well as the virtues of this poetry, are my own; and no other person could possibly lay hands upon any poem of mine in order to correct some real or imagined error without harming the poem more seriously than any faulty execution of my own could possibly have done.[37]

Her poetry reiterates this insistence upon the absolute integrity of the artist's work:

Such as I am, however, I have brought
To what it is, this tower; it is my own;
Though it was reared to Beauty, it was wrought
With what I had to build with:

the necessity of the poet's giving all he has to his work—

Still as of old his being give
In Beauty's name, while she may live. . . .

. . . his empathy with the suffering of the world—

> The anguish of the world is on my tongue.
> My bowl is filled to the brim with it; there is more
> > than I can eat.

. . . his constant awareness of the beauty underlying the ugly, the sordid, and the mean—

> As sharp as in my childhood, still
> Ecstasy shocks me fixed.

. . . all qualities which make up his unique vision must, when they are finally given form in language, be allowed to stand as written, whether or not they are understood or appreciated. "I have learned to fail," Vincent Millay wrote with characteristic honesty, in "Lines Written in Recapitulation." But she also, at times, succeeded magnificently; that she refused to be influenced by "The Waste Land" and its imitations is rather more to her credit than otherwise.

For she could not imitate the gloom-filled, direly prophetic poetry which became the fashion after 1922. Although she wrote of grief and loneliness, though humanity sometimes disillusioned her, nevertheless her poetry is permeated with an unshatterable belief in the intrinsic goodness of the world. She clung, as all humanity must, to her ideal of the human spirit at its highest and best. From the first glad acceptance of "Renascence," to the last poems in *Mine The Harvest*, there is a recurrent appeal to man to rejoice in life, and to accept its challenge:

> We, we the living, we the still alive—
> Why, what a triumph, what a task is here!

And the task? "To build our world; if not this year, next year." In one of her last poems, "Journal," she addresses herself to future generations in most persuasive words:

> Oh, children, growing up to be
> Adventurers into sophistry,
> Forbear, forbear to be of those

That read the root to learn the rose;
Whose thoughts are like a tugging kite,
Anchored by day, drawn in at night.
Grieve not if from the mind be loosed
A wing that comes not home to roost;
There may be garnered yet of that
An olive-branch from Ararat.

She genuinely feared an over-rationalistic approach to life, lest it deaden the spirit:

We are clever,—we are clever as monkeys, and some of us
Have intellect, which is our danger, for we lack intelligence
And have forgotten instinct.

It was to the preservation of intelligence and instinct, and to the destruction of cynicism and *acidie* that poetry called her:

Yet I shall sing until my voice crack (this being my leisure, this my
holiday)
That man was a special thing and no commodity, a thing improper
to be sold.

Life *is* transient and fleeting, but, so far as she was concerned, it should be lived "with all my senses, well aware/That this was perfect, and it would not last." Sorrow must be accepted, for in it strength can be found; even death can be kind, "reminding us how much we dared to love." Perhaps Edna St. Vincent Millay's vision can best be summed up in the final stanza of "Small Hands, Relinquish All":

Only the ardent eye,
Only the listening ear
Can say, "The thrush was here!"
Can say, "His song was clear!"
Can live, before it die.

The new reader, encountering her poetry for the first time, can agree with the comment of Edmund Wilson: "One never forgot the things she noticed, for she charged them with her own intensest feeling. This power of enhancing and ennobling life was felt by all who knew her." [38] In an age when there is so much chatter about idealism and the inviolability of the human spirit, it may be that the poetry of Edna St. Vincent Millay may prove a delightful, heartening discovery.

Footnotes

Unless otherwise noted, all references are to Miriam Gurko, *Restless Spirit: The Life of Edna St. Vincent Millay*, Crowell, 1962 (Gurko), and to *Letters of Edna St. Vincent Millay*, edited by Allan Ross Macdougall, Grosset and Dunlap, 1952 (Letters).

Poems taken from *Collected Poems: Edna St. Vincent Millay*, edited by Norma Millay, Harper & Row, publishers, 1956.

[1] *Letters*, 71
[2] Gurko, 238
[3] *Letters*, 350
[4] *Ibid.*, 118
[5] *Ibid.*, 9
[6] *Ibid.*
[7] Gurko, 23
[8] *Ibid.*, 47
[9] *Letters*, 20
[10] *Ibid.*
[11] *Ibid.*, 36
[12] *Ibid.*, 37
[13] Notation by Norma Millay Ellis
[14] Gurko, 58
[15] *Letters*, 48
[16] *Ibid.*, 52
[17] Gurko, 71
[18] Everett Shinn, conversation with author, spring, 1952.
[19] Edmund Wilson, *The Shores of Light* (Farrar, Straus and Young), 1952, 752–3.

[20] *Letters*, 245
[21] *Ibid.*, 106
[22] *Ibid.*
[23] *Ibid.*, 168
[24] *Ibid.*, 174
[25] John Hall Wheelock, conversation with author.
[26] Gurko, 154
[27] *Ibid.*, 169
[28] *Ibid.*
[29] *Letters*, 240
[30] *Ibid.*, 312
[31] *Ibid.*
[32] *Ibid.*
[33] *Ibid.*, 374
[34] Gurko, 256
[35] Marianne Moore, conversation with author.
[36] *Letters*, 341
[37] *Ibid.*, 329
[38] Wilson, 475

Poems

Renascence

All I could see from where I stood
Was three long mountains and a wood;
I turned and looked another way,
And saw three islands in a bay.
So with my eyes I traced the line
Of the horizon, thin and fine,
Straight around till I was come
Back to where I'd started from;
And all I saw from where I stood
Was three long mountains and a wood.

Over these things I could not see:
These were the things that bounded me.
And I could touch them with my hand,
Almost, I thought, from where I stand!
And all at once things seemed so small
My breath came short, and scarce at all.
But, sure, the sky is big, I said:
Miles and miles above my head.
So here upon my back I'll lie
And look my fill into the sky.
And so I looked, and after all,
The sky was not so very tall.
The sky, I said, must somewhere stop . . .
And—sure enough!—I see the top!
The sky, I thought, is not so grand;
I 'most could touch it with my hand!
And reaching up my hand to try,
I screamed, to feel it touch the sky.

I screamed, and—lo!—Infinity
Came down and settled over me;
Forced back my scream into my chest;
Bent back my arm upon my breast;
And, pressing of the Undefined
The definition on my mind,
Held up before my eyes a glass
Through which my shrinking sight did pass
Until it seemed I must behold
Immensity made manifold;
Whispered to me a word whose sound
Deafened the air for worlds around,
And brought unmuffled to my ears
The gossiping of friendly spheres,
The creaking of the tented sky,
The ticking of Eternity.

I saw and heard, and knew at last
The How and Why of all things, past,
And present, and forevermore.
The Universe, cleft to the core,
Lay open to my probing sense,
That, sickening, I would fain pluck thence
But could not,—nay! but needs must suck
At that great wound, and could not pluck
My lips away till I had drawn
All venom out.—Ah, fearful pawn:
For my omniscience paid I toll
In infinite remorse of soul.
All sin was of my sinning, all
Atoning mine, and mine the gall
Of all regret. Mine was the weight
Of every brooded wrong, the hate
That stood behind each envious thrust,
Mine every greed, mine every lust.

And all the while, for every grief,

Each suffering, I craved relief
With individual desire;
Craved all in vain! And felt fierce fire
About a thousand people crawl;
Perished with each,—then mourned for all!

A man was starving in Capri;
He moved his eyes and looked at me;
I felt his gaze, I heard his moan,
And knew his hunger as my own.
I saw at sea a great fog bank
Between two ships that struck and sank;
A thousand screams the heavens smote;
And every scream tore through my throat.

No hurt I did not feel, no death
That was not mine; mine each last breath
That, crying, met an answering cry
From the compassion that was I.
All suffering mine, and mine its rod;
Mine, pity like the pity of God.

Ah, awful weight! Infinity
Pressed down upon the finite Me!
My anguished spirit, like a bird,
Beating against my lips I heard;
Yet lay the weight so close about
There was no room for it without.
And so beneath the weight lay I
And suffered death, but could not die.

Long had I lain thus, craving death,
When quietly the earth beneath
Gave way, and inch by inch, so great
At last had grown the crushing weight,
Into the earth I sank till I
Full six feet under ground did lie,
And sank no more,—there is no weight

Can follow here, however great.
From off my breast I felt it roll,
And as it went my tortured soul
Burst forth and fled in such a gust
That all about me swirled the dust.

Deep in the earth I rested now.
Cool is its hand upon the brow
And soft its breast beneath the head
Of one who is so gladly dead.
And all at once, and over all
The pitying rain began to fall;
I lay and heard each pattering hoof
Upon my lowly, thatchèd roof,
And seemed to love the sound far more
Than ever I had done before.
For rain it hath a friendly sound
To one who's six feet under ground;
And scarce the friendly voice or face,
A grave is such a quiet place.

The rain, I said, is kind to come
And speak to me in my new home.
I would I were alive again
To kiss the fingers of the rain,
To drink into my eyes the shine
Of every slanting silver line,
To catch the freshened, fragrant breeze
From drenched and dripping apple-trees.
For soon the shower will be done,
And then the broad face of the sun
Will laugh above the rain-soaked earth
Until the world with answering mirth
Shakes joyously, and each round drop
Rolls, twinkling, from its grass-blade top.
How can I bear it, buried here,
While overhead the sky grows clear

And blue again after the storm?
O, multi-coloured, multi-form,
Belovèd beauty over me,
That I shall never, never see
Again! Spring-silver, autumn-gold,
That I shall never more behold!—
Sleeping your myriad magics through,
Close-sepulchred away from you!
O God, I cried, give me new birth,
And put me back upon the earth!
Upset each cloud's gigantic gourd
And let the heavy rain, down-poured
In one big torrent, set me free,
Washing my grave away from me!

I ceased; and through the breathless hush
That answered me, the far-off rush
Of herald wings came whispering
Like music down the vibrant spring
Of my ascending prayer, and—crash!
Before the wild wind's whistling lash
The startled storm-clouds reared on high
And plunged in terror down the sky!
And the big rain in one black wave
Fell from the sky and struck my grave.

I know not how such things can be;
I only know there came to me
A fragrance such as never clings
To aught save happy living things;
A sound as of some joyous elf
Singing sweet songs to please himself,
And, through and over everything,
A sense of glad awakening.
The grass, a-tiptoe at my ear,

Whispering to me I could hear;
I felt the rain's cool finger-tips
Brushed tenderly across my lips,
Laid gently on my sealèd sight,
And all at once the heavy night
Fell from my eyes and I could see!—
A drenched and dripping apple-tree,
A last long line of silver rain,
A sky grown clear and blue again.
And as I looked a quickening gust
Of wind blew up to me and thrust
Into my face a miracle
Of orchard-breath, and with the smell,—
I know not how such things can be!—
I breathed my soul back into me.

Ah! Up then from the ground sprang I
And hailed the earth with such a cry
As is not heard save from a man
Who has been dead, and lives again.
About the trees by arms I wound;
Like one gone mad I hugged the ground;
I raised my quivering arms on high;
I laughed and laughed into the sky;
Till at my throat a strangling sob
Caught fiercely, and a great heart-throb
Sent instant tears into my eyes:
O God, I cried, no dark disguise
Can e'er hereafter hide from me
Thy radiant identity!
Thou canst not move across the grass
But my quick eyes will see Thee pass,
Nor speak, however silently,
But my hushed voice will answer Thee.

I know the path that tells Thy way
Through the cool eve of every day;
God, I can push the grass apart
And lay my finger on Thy heart!

The world stands out on either side
No wider than the heart is wide;
Above the world is stretched the sky,—
No higher than the soul is high.
The heart can push the sea and land
Farther away on either hand;
The soul can split the sky in two,
And let the face of God shine through.
But East and West will pinch the heart
That cannot keep them pushed apart;
And he whose soul is flat—the sky
Will cave in on him by and by.

Afternoon on a Hill

I will be the gladdest thing
    Under the sun!
I will touch a hundred flowers
    And not pick one.

I will look at cliffs and clouds
    With quiet eyes,
Watch the wind bow down the grass,
    And the grass rise.

And when the lights begin to show
    Up from town,
I will mark which must be mine,
    And then start down!

From *"Renascence" and Other Poems*

To the Not Impossible Him

How shall I know, unless I go
    To Cairo and Cathay,
Whether or not this blessèd spot
    Is blest in every way?

Now it may be, the flower for me
    Is this beneath my nose;
How shall I tell, unless I smell
    The Carthaginian rose?

The fabric of my faithful love
    No power shall dim or ravel
Whilst I stay here,—but oh, my dear,
    If I should ever travel!

From A *Few Figs from Thistles*

Sonnets

Oh, think not I am faithful to a vow!
Faithless am I save to love's self alone.
Were you not lovely I would leave you now:
After the feet of beauty fly my own.
Were you not still my hunger's rarest food,
And water ever to my wildest thirst,
I would desert you—think not but I would!—
And seek another as I sought you first.
But you are mobile as the veering air,
And all your charms more changeful than the tide,
Wherefore to be inconstant is no care:
I have but to continue at your side.
So wanton, light and false, my love, are you,
I am most faithless when I most am true.

From A *Few Figs from Thistles*

Those hours when happy hours were my estate,—
Entailed, as proper, for the next in line,
Yet mine the harvest, and the title mine—
Those acres, fertile, and the furrow straight,
From which the lark would rise—all of my late
Enchantments, still, in brilliant colours, shine,
But striped with black, the tulip, lawn, and vine,
Like gardens looked at through an iron gate.
Yet not as one who never sojourned there
I view the lovely segments of a past
I lived with all my senses, well aware
That this was perfect, and it would not last:
I smell the flower, though vacuum-still the air;
I feel its texture, though the gate is fast.

From *Mine the Harvest*

Euclid alone has looked on Beauty bare.
Let all who prate of Beauty hold their peace,
And lay them prone upon the earth and cease
To ponder on themselves, the while they stare
At nothing, intricately drawn nowhere
In shapes of shifting lineage; let geese
Gabble and hiss, but heroes seek release
From dusty bondage into luminous air.
O blinding hour, O holy, terrible day,
When first the shaft into his vision shone
Of light anatomized! Euclid alone
Has looked on Beauty bare. Fortunate they
Who, though once only and then but far away,
Have heard her massive sandal set on stone.

From *The Harp Weaver*

Marianne Moore

1887-

*"Of poetry, I once said, 'I, too, dislike it'; and
say it again of anything mannered, dictatorial,
disparaging, or calculated to reduce to the ranks
what offends one. I have been accused of
substituting appreciation for criticism and justly,
since there is nothing I dislike more than the
exposé or any kind of revenge."* [1]
QUERY: *"Miss Moore, what do you consider the
raison d'être of poetry?"*
REPLY: *"Precisely what Cicero thought—to
fascinate, instruct, and to stir the mind."* [2]

*S*HE enchants. She is poetry itself. And on November 15,
1968, all the news media paused in their hectic recital of the
days events, the war in Viet Nam, post mortems on the meaning
of the election, and the latest campus demonstration, to record
an event that was as delightful as it was expected, and quite as
important to the world as rumors of summit conferences and
peace talks in Paris. The National Book Committee announced
that the recipient of its 1968 National Medal for Literature was
Miss Marianne Moore.

The committee's citation which accompanied the award is
worth quotation, because it provides a marvellous introduction
not only to her poetry, but also to the poet herself: "In her lively
art, peacocks, snails, steamrollers, unicorns, nectarines, granite
and steel—all evoke enchanted glimpses of eternity." "Indeed,"
Miss Moore replied, "That's a big claim. I'm not Columbus
discovering America, you know. I'm a worker with words, that's
all." [3] True enough, she *is* a worker with words. But, as she says
in one of her poems,

> Yes, light is speech. Free frank
> impartial sunlight, moonlight,

185

starlight, lighthouse light
are language.

Language is the poet's special medium. The function of language is communication, but the poet is the unique interpreter endowed with the gift of carrying language far beyond communication to illumination. By this definition, Marianne Moore is certainly the poet chosen for the hour, despite her modest disclaimer that ". . . if I write what is called poetry, it is because there is no other category in which to put it." [4]

Similarly she disclaims any "literary ancestry" which might have influenced her to become a poet. Born in Kirkwood, a suburb of St. Louis, Missouri, on November 15, 1887—that November 15, 1968 was her eighty-first birthday is a matter of delightful indifference to her!—she grew up in the home of her grandfather, the Reverend John R. Warner, pastor of the First Presbyterian Church of Kirkwood at the same time that T. S. Eliot's grandfather was pastor of the Unitarian Church of St. Louis. (The families did not know each other, however, nor were the Moores acquainted with the Teasdales, whose daughter Sara was three years younger than Marianne.)

Marianne Moore's father, John Milton Moore, was an engineer who had wanted to manufacture a smokeless furnace; his failure to achieve his dream had resulted in a nervous breakdown, and with his brother he had returned to his own family in Portsmouth, Ohio, before his daughter's birth. Her reticence concerning her father is to be respected, but this much may be surmised—some of her scientific bent, which led to her enthusiasm for courses in biology as a college student, is probably inherited, as well as her tremendous interest in architectural structure evidenced in poems such as "Granite and Steel," and in the exclamation "Neatness of finish! Neatness of finish!" which startles the first-time reader of "The Octopus."

A more readily discernible influence was that of her mother, Mary Warner Moore, of whom she wrote in her postscript to *Selected Poems:*

In my immediate family there is one who thinks "in a particular way;" and I should like to think that where there is an effect of thought or pith in these pages, the thinking and often the actual phrases were hers.[5]

In her famous interview with Donald Hall, published in *The Paris Review* for Winter, 1961, she tells how she asked her mother's opinion of a poem and her mother remarked succinctly, "It won't do." And that was all. No why or wherefore— simply, "It won't do." On another occasion, when Marianne asked her why she had ever permitted her to publish a particular poem, she replied, "You didn't ask my advice." [6] Certainly Mrs. Moore must have possessed what the Irish call "a gift for words"; and in the poem "Spenser's Ireland," in the line, "I'm troubled, I'm dissatisfied, I'm Irish," Marianne recognizes and, incidentally, reveals a probable source for her own fascination with perfection in language. Too, as a small girl in a preacher's household in the late eighties and early nineties, at a time when sermons were supposed to be rhetorically effective, as well as sincerely religious, she must have unconsciously absorbed not only many ideas about rhetoric, composition, and—to use one of her descriptive words—"precision," but also that most important quality in poetry, the *sound* of language beautifully spoken.

Marianne's grandfather died in 1894, and her mother after taking the children to Carlisle, Pennsylvania, to live was persuaded to become an English teacher at Metzger Institute, a girls' school which has since become a part of Dickinson College. In Carlisle, Marianne and her elder brother Warner (who was later to follow in his grandfather's footsteps and become a minister) went to school. She graduated from Metzger Institute in 1905, and that autumn entered Bryn Mawr College. She had hoped to major in English and French, but her language preparation was inadequate—she had never spoken French!—and, though she had read widely in a variety of authors, she could not meet Bryn Mawr's pre-requisites for taking elective courses until her junior year. Strangely enough, it was Marianne's writing that was the problem; telling of a certain professor's returning an essay with the comment, "Miss Moore, I presume you had an idea, if one could find out what it is!" she comments herself, now, with a rueful shake of her head, "That was cruel, wasn't it!" [7] But originality, especially in writing, unless it is the professor's particular brand of originality, is not always prized; Marianne Moore was not the only student to learn that, in some classrooms, when an irresistible force meets an immovable object, something has to give.

Nevertheless, she loved Bryn Mawr. It was exciting to be on a college campus, especially one presided over by the legendary M. Carey Thomas, whose battle for women's right to an education equivalent to the one that their brothers enjoyed at Harvard and Yale is one of the unsung epics of educational history. It has been said that Miss Thomas customarily perused the Harvard and Yale entrance examinations, then deliberately designed Bryn Mawr's to be more difficult. It is a fact that nothing ever prevented her from performing her duties as president; even when a broken leg forced her to remain away from her office, she received her faculty members, staff, and college guests propped up on pillows in her enormous canopied bed, wearing her academic gown. Constantly she urged her "Bryn Mawrtyrs" to realize that "It is not the narrowness of our horizon, but it is the narrowness of our gaze that defeats us." All her efforts were directed to widening that gaze (by force, if necessary!), not only to intellectual and cultural pursuits, but also to the call of the world beyond the college walls, and to the responsibility of educated women for answering that call. She was both an inspiration and a goad to the young women who came under her sway—"living in another world from that of 'half happiness,' 'half love,' and 'the little little poems that were being written,'" [8] Marianne Moore wrote of her, and she freely admits that M. Carey Thomas of Bryn Mawr played an important role in helping her to form her own convictions and sense of commitment.

In one of her delightful prose pieces, "If I were Sixteen Today," Marianne Moore avers that she felt decidedly insecure as a teenager, that she considered herself a wallflower. Her graduation photograph in the Bryn Mawr 1909 *Yearbook* belies these assertions, however. Her expression is rather serious and pensive, and her coronet braid is simplicity itself beside the elaborate puffs and curls of her classmates. She *is* uniquely different, and lovely, as she is today. The pleated shirtwaist with its high, boned collar cannot vitiate the glint of humor in her eyes; the class poem mentions especially her gift of laughter. That she reacted as any normal college student occasionally did, and still does, to high intellectual demands is evident from the following comment in the same essay: "Instead of hating an over-heavy curriculum . . . I would give thought to the why rather than merely the what of a subject." [9] She also gives one very sage piece of advice: "To the postponers I would say, DO IT NOW; and to firebrands of impatience, ROME WAS NOT BUILT IN A DAY." [10]

The paradox seemingly inherent in this statement dissolves when the reader begins to understand what Marianne Moore unequivocally believes: procrastinators by their very nature need extra prodding, and firebrands need a tighter rein, so that both may reach the precise golden mean. What Bryn Mawr meant to her in essence, and what she feels the college experience does and should continue to mean, is the experience of being thrust into an ambiance where one, hopefully, learns the wholesome if frightening truth that

> . . . it may be that we
> have not knowledge, just opinions, that we are
> undergraduates,
> not students;

and is forced to recognize certain inevitable facts of existence which must be accepted with grace:

> You can't beat hens to
> make them lay. Wolf's wool is the best of wool,
> but it cannot be sheared because
> the wolf will not comply.

Two important discoveries that can be devastating if too long delayed!

Her poem of 1966, written in honor of Dr. Katherine Mc-Bride's twenty-fifth anniversary as president of Bryn Mawr, holds both her own retrospective attitude towards her college years, and a challenge for the future of those who teach and learn within all "ivy-covered walls":

What is a college? *
a place where freedom is rooted in vitality,
where faith is the substance of things hoped for,
where things seen were not made with hands—
where the school's initiator being dead, yet speaketh,
where virtue trod a rough and thorny path,
finding itself and losing itself—
the student her own taskmaster,
tenacious of one hour's meaning sought
that could not be found elsewhere.[11]

Immediately following her graduation, she took a secretarial course at Carlisle College; then, from 1911 to 1915, she taught stenography, typing, bookkeeping, English, and law at the United States Industrial Indian School at Carlisle. "I knew nothing about bookkeeping," she says with an eloquent sigh. "I used to send the problems to my brother at Princeton, and he'd work them and send them back. Wasn't that good of him?" [12] She admits quite as candidly to knowing even less about law, having taken only a course at Bryn Mawr given by Dean Ashley. She sometimes after school watched the boys in field sports; one of her students was Jim Thorpe, eventually to become a famous all-around athlete and winner of the decathlon at the Olympic Games of 1912. But she did not find this kind of teaching inspiring, and felt no regret at leaving it in 1916 when her brother, having been ordained to the ministry, asked her to come with her mother to Chatham, New Jersey, to live with him. The Moores stayed in Chatham for two years;

* "What is a College?" by Cornelia Meigs

when America entered World War I, Warner went into the navy as a chaplain, and Marianne and her mother took an apartment in Greenwich Village.

It was about this time that she seriously began to write poetry. She had done some writing for the Bryn Mawr undergraduate magazine, *Tipyn O'Bob,* and had served on the editorial staff; and she had also contributed a few prose pieces to the alumnae magazine, *The Lantern.* Poetry, at that time, had not called her. Her interest in it came slowly, first through her fascination with words and rhythm—much intrigued by metrical patterns. She wrote, sent her work to magazines, collecting rejection slips along the way, but in 1915 *The Egoist,* an English magazine devoted to Imagist Poetry, published her "To Military Progress." In May of that same year, five of her poems appeared in *Poetry.* Harriet Monroe has described them quite aptly as "elliptically whimsical profundities;" [13] they are short, direct, charming, and indicate clearly the direction of the poet's future work. For instance, "The Wizard in Words"—

> "When I am dead,"
> The wizard said,
> "I'll look upon the narrow way,
> And this Dante,
>   And know that he was right;
>   And he'll delight
>   In my remorse—
>   Of Course."

> "When I am dead,"
> The student said,
> "I shall have grown so tolerant
> I'll find I can't
>   Laugh at your sorry plight,
>   Or take delight
>   In your chagrin,
>   Merlin."

This has all the allusiveness which fascinates, and of necessity instructs, for if the reader cannot call to mind the Sermon on the Mount, Tennyson's "Merlin and Vivien" and Dante's *Divina Commedia*, he must learn what these sources contain to appreciate fully the depth of the poem. The main point is clear —the wizard has used his power over language for wrong, while Dante has used his to glorify God; the student, struggling to make words "work" at all, finds it impossible to do otherwise than sympathize with a successful practitioner of the art, even though the end to which it has been directed is in error. Or, is the student's "tolerance" to be taken as the poet's ironic comment on the decidedly less-than-genius who accepts anything as long as it is published? This poem demonstrates that, even in her earliest work, Marianne Moore was capable of stirring the mind. The form of the poem has some kinship with imagism, but the poet emphatically denies any influence of that school; and, indeed, to read "The Wizard in Words" in conjunction with the work of Aldington, Pound, or H.D. is to discover that the Moore poem is completely different in approach. It comments on, rather than "images" experience.

From 1918 to 1921, Marianne worked as a secretary in a girls' school and also did some tutoring, then she accepted a job as a parttime assistant in the Hudson Park Branch of the New York Public Library. "Working as a librarian was a help, a tremendous help," she has said about that interlude. "As a free service we were assigned books to review and I did like that. We didn't get paid, but we had the chance to diagnose. I reveled in it." [14]

Even though most of the books were what she described as "silent-movie fiction," she believes that the task of reviewing them helped to "harden" her mental approach to writing. For by now she was actively and ardently writing. Prior to 1916 she had known no writers; even though Hilda Doolittle had been her college classmate, she had not realized at that time that H.D. was interested in poetry. But publication in *The Egoist* and *Poetry* brought her into contact with a group of poets who were then living and working in New York.

The unofficial leader of the group was Alfred Kreymborg,

editor of a magazine of contemporary poetry called *Others*; William Carlos Williams, Conrad Aiken, and Wallace Stevens were also members. Marianne Moore quickly found her own place in this company; her wit and remarkable "gift for words" enchanted and delighted them. "Marianne was our saint—if we had one—in whom we all instinctively felt our purpose come together to form a stream," William Carlos Williams has written. "Everyone loved her." [15] Even more important, they respected her as a poet; so did Ezra Pound, though he did query, "What the devil of your punctuation?" and T. S. Eliot, who wrote, ". . . I can only, at the moment, think of five contemporary poets—English, Irish, American, French, and German—whose work excites me as much as, or more, than Miss Moore's." [16] In 1920, two of her poems—"England," and "Picking and Choosing"—appeared in *The Dial*; and in 1921, without her knowledge for she would have prevented them had she known, a volume of her poems culled from various magazines was published in England under the sponsorship of H.D. and Winifred Ellerman, better known to the American reading public today as the brilliant historical novelist "Bryher." Despite Marianne's own feeling that the book was premature—"a slight product, conspicuously tentative," she has called it—[17] and that she was not yet ready for such definitive publication, others did not agree. Early in 1922, *Poetry* devoted an entire issue to a symposium on her work, and in 1924, her first important volume, *Observations*, received the *Dial* Award.

The $2,000 which accompanied this prize was naturally very welcome, but even more important was the recognition it brought to the recipient. *The Dial* was known to have exceedingly high standards; it did not bestow its praise lightly. The editors sought to attract the best to its pages—Marianne was already there, so they invited her to join the staff. She consented, even though it meant neglecting her own work, because she possesses an unusual quality—a highly developed sense of gratitude. Many can testify to this grace in her, which leads her to view the slightest kindness as an opportunity to do something for the person performing it, as if the performance of it were not already honor enough. Her gratitude will not be deflected; protests are declined with a firm, quiet, "This is unseemly! I *wish* to express my affection."

So it was with *The Dial;* the magazine had honored her, and now offered her a way to show her appreciation. In July, 1925, she became acting editor; the following year she was the editor, and those years from 1926 to 1929, when the magazine ceased publication, were its *anni mirabiles.* To look through its files is to view a panorama of arts and letters of the Twenties. Ezra Pound and George Saintsbury, a most incongruous combination, both appeared in the same issue; D. H. Lawrence, Bertrand Russell, Padraic Colum, Hart Crane, Thomas Mann, Gertrude Stein, John Dos Passos, Llewelyn Powys—the list is as varied as it is endless. Reproductions of paintings by Picasso, Matisse, and Chagall stand side by side with articles by Marianne Moore which perceptively and incisively discuss the newcomers to the literary ranks. Why was *The Dial* so remarkable? Marianne Moore's own words provide the answer:

> Lack of fear, for one thing . . . I never knew a magazine that was so self-propulsive. Everybody liked what he was doing, and when we made grievous mistakes we were sorry, but we laughed over them. . . .
> I think individuality was the great thing. We were not conforming to anything. We certainly didn't have a policy, except I remember hearing the word 'intensity' very often. A thing must have 'intensity.' That seemed to be the criterion.[18]

It should be noted in passing that this kind of situation could be possible only with a group of people who were both thoroughly knowledgeable concerning their craft, and sufficiently self-disciplined to recognize that there is no merit in nonconformity for its own sake. Individuality is not the same thing as egotism. The work published in *The Dial* under Marianne Moore's editorship almost without exception possessed that quality so beautifully described in her poem "When I Buy Pictures"—a criterion which she would also apply to poetry:

> It comes to this: of whatever sort it is,
> It must be "lit with piercing glances into the life of things,"
> It must acknowledge the spiritual forces which have made it.

Those who are able to accomplish this can be safely allowed to be nonconformists, for they can be assumed to have sound reasons for breaking with traditional methods of poetic diction. They are not like the "Novices," who traffic with:

> an abstruse idea plain to none but the artist,
> the only seller who buys and holds on to the money.
> Because one expresses oneself and entitles it wisdom,
> one is not a fool. What an idea!

Nor will they fall into the snare of complexity for the sake of complexity, as though the merit of a poem could be reckoned in direct ratio to its obscurity:

> . . . complexity is not a crime, but carry
> it to the point of murkiness
> and nothing is plain. Complexity
> moreover, that has been committed to darkness instead of
> granting itself to be the pestilence that it is, moves all a-
> bout as if to bewilder us with the dismal
> fallacy that insistence
> is the measure of achievement and that all
> truth must be dark.

"Insistence" is not a synonym for "intensity."

The demands of editorship were enormous; Marianne had said that she would take the job if she didn't have to write letters or see contributors, but very quickly she found herself doing both. To this day, she insists that the decision to cease publication was "largely chivalry" on the part of the chief backers of *The Dial*, because her work for the magazine had brought her own writing almost to a standstill. In any case, the end of her tenure as editor came perhaps as a blessing in disguise; her mother was ill and needed her care. Her brother by now was stationed at Brooklyn Navy Yard, so she moved to Brooklyn in the autumn of 1929, to a house on Clinton Hill, in a city marked by the decorum she prizes, where trees still grew—"massive branches of elms with the anatomy of oaks—" [19] and maids in starched white aprons served afternoon tea.

Here, she returned again to the writer's special joy, her own work. *Selected Poems*, with an introduction by T. S. Eliot was published in 1935; *"The Pangolin" and Other Verse* in 1936; *What Are Years* in 1941; *Nevertheless* in 1944; *Collected Poems* in 1951; *Like a Bulwark* in 1956; *O To Be a Dragon* in 1959; *Tell Me, Tell Me* in 1966; and *Complete Poems* in 1967. *Predilections*, a collection of her prose essays, appeared in 1955; she collaborated with Elizabeth Meyer in a translation of Adalbert Stifter's beautiful Christmas story, *Rock Crystal*, in 1945, and in 1954 published her own version of *The Fables of La Fontaine*. She has also contributed, and continues to contribute, articles and book reviews to numerous magazines—as well as poems which, it is to be hoped, will soon be collected into a new volume.

The great honors which have been conferred upon her are almost overwhelming to contemplate. In 1940, she won the Shelley Memorial Award; in 1944, the Contemporary Poetry Patrons' Prize and the Harriet Monroe Poetry Award. The Guggenheim Foundation awarded her a fellowship in 1945; in 1946 she received a joint grant from the American Academy of Arts and Letters and the National Institute of Arts and Letters. Wilson College, Mt. Holyoke, Smith, the University of Rochester, Rutgers, Dickinson College, Long Island University, and Pratt Institute have granted her honorary degrees; in 1947, she was elected to the National Institute of Arts and Letters.

The year 1952 was truly the *annus mirabilis*—she received the National Book Award for poetry, the Pulitzer Prize, and the Bollingen Prize. In 1953, she won the gold medal for poetry from the National Institute of Arts and Letters, and the

M. Carey Thomas Award from a committee of colleges; and, as has already been mentioned, 1968 brought the National Book Committee medal.

Honors, however, though greatly appreciated, rest with lightness upon the shoulders of this *très grande dame*—who does not bear the remotest resemblance to the "dear little old lady" a national magazine (perhaps intending to be humorous) recently referred to, as a description of her. Wearing the black tricorne hat because she likes it—"Fashion," she maintains, "can make you ridiculous; style, which is yours to control individually, can make you attractive—a near siren" [20]—she appears at the most glittering social functions, and is invariably a center of attention. Television viewers, who have seen her on the *Today* and *Tonight* shows, testify delightedly to her charm which can disarm the most tenaciously professional cynic.

All this acclaim, however, she treats with gentle humor—never, with deprecation—and with a sense of proportion, too. She prizes a baseball autographed by the New York Yankees, given to her by Michael Burke, president of the Yankees, after she threw the first ball of the season in 1968, caught by Frank Fernandez, as highly as her gold medals. To the Ford Motor Company's request in 1955 that she try to devise a name for a new car, which eventually turned out to be the Edsel (the entire correspondence, reprinted in A *Marianne Moore Reader*, must be read *in toto* to be fully appreciated), she brought all the "precision, economy of statement, logic employed to ends that are disinterested" [21] that she would bring to a poem, and enjoyed herself hugely into the bargain. "That seemed to me a very worthy pursuit," she commented. "I am interested in mechanics, mechanics in general. And I enjoyed the assignment, for all that it was abortive." And the Edsel itself? "It was a very handsome car. It came out in the wrong year." [22]

Marianne Moore herself is the supreme exemplification of her own creed for poetry: "Humility, Concentration, and Gusto."

Analyzing her poetry has become a kind of indoor sport for many critics, professional and amateur. The "sport" she approves, but attempts at analysis disturb her, because,

>   Writing is exacting
>   and baseball is like writing.
>   You can never tell with either
>   how it will go
>   or what you will do.

Critical attempts to find "hidden meanings" she greets with gentle exasperation, because she says what she means, and means what she says. "Always, in whatever I wrote—prose or verse—I have had a burning desire to be explicit," [23] for,

>   . . . we
>   do not admire what
>   we cannot understand.

But her own search for meaning sometimes proves a Herculean quest: "I doubt that anyone who is incurably interested in writing as I am, and always doing it, has had as much difficulty as I have in expressing what I am fanatically determined to say." [24] Occasionally she has been criticized for incorporating direct quotations from other writers into her poems; her calm response is, "When a thing has been said so well that it could not be said better, why paraphrase it?" [25] And, as any Bryn Mawrtyr will affirm, four years of adamant professorial "Cite the source" requirements, with no mercy shown to quite unintentional, inadvertent plagiarism, make an indelible impression! The quotations in her poetry are Marianne Moore's way of sharing the thoughts and ideas which have been of comfort and pleasure to her.

They also emphasize the truth of her assertion that "I think books are chiefly responsible for my doggedly self-determined efforts to write," [26] an assertion which the living room of her New York apartment confirms. (She left Brooklyn in the spring of 1968 because Clinton Hill had changed so radically that she no longer felt at home there.) It is a pleasant, comfortable room, which she herself graces. Bookshelves line a long wall extending into the entrance hall; in the room itself books overflow onto a round coffee table before, and the end-table beside, the sofa. Books are piled on the ledges below the long windows. The latest volumes of poetry, fascinating catalogues from art exhibits, and a new book on needlepoint rest comfortably beside the autographed baseball and a manual on boxing! Books are on the writing table; on the wall above it hang an engraving of a portrait of Robert Burns and three reproductions from William Blake's *Jerusalem*. The visitor knows instantly, too, that all the books have been, are being, and will be read and reread. "Feed the imagination with food that invigorates," [27] Marianne Moore says, in one of her delightful essays. Definitely in this she follows her own advice; in conversation she quotes verbatim from Robert Browning (whom she considers a "cornerstone of culture" [28]) Henry James, Shakespeare, Chaucer, Martin Buber, and the Book of Job, to mention a few, and from others as they seem pertinent to the topic being discussed.

Her poetry, for all its untraditional form, nevertheless reveals full knowledge of the traditions of the past; her technique is firmly rooted in complete understanding of the poet's craft. When she breaks the "rules," she knows *how* to break them, and, even more important, *why* she is breaking them. Thus her poems have an authority of tone, even while they are most daringly experimental. Her emphasis on the "instruction" element in poetry, along with "fascinating" (which she places first) and "stirring the mind," makes her work seem at times to hold a special kinship with the eighteenth century. She admits to the specific influence of eighteenth century prose, especially that of Samuel Johnson and Edmund Burke, and the eighteenth century dictum of "what oft was thought, but ne'er so well expressed," is certainly applicable as well. Lines such as:

> The translucent mistake
> of the desert, does not make

hardship for one who
can rest and then do
the opposite. . . .

or:

Discreet behaviour is not now the sum
of statesmanlike good sense.
Though
it were the incarnation of dead grace?
As if a death mask could replace
life's faulty excellence.

or the marvelous lines in "Marriage," which she describes as "a
little anthology of statements that took my fancy—phrasings
that I liked": [29]

he loves himself so much,
he can permit himself
no rival in that love.
She loves herself so much,
she cannot see herself enough.

convey the wit, and "point" with commonsense, so praised by
Alexander Pope, in twentieth century terms.

Another quality of her poetry which is reminiscent of the
eighteenth century attitude is the urbanity which accompanies
her social comment. "Talent, knowledge, humility, reverence,
magnanimity, involve the inconvenience of responsibility, or
they die." [30] "Responsibility" in this context means to be con-
sistently kind. Damning out of hand or with faint praise is
malicious, and—even worse in Marianne Moore's opinion—of
no use to the world. "Blessed is the man," she writes,

who does not sit in the seat of the scoffer—
the man who does not denigrate, depreciate, denunciate;
who is not "characteristically intemperate,"
who does not "excuse, retreat, equivocate; and will be heard."

Magnanimity, however, is not to be confused with superficial,
sentimental "tolerance" of error, stupidity, or wrong. She can

use a rapier with effect. In the same poem she adds with her incisive wit:

> Blessed are the geniuses who know
> that egomania is not a duty.

In "Marriage," wondering what Adam and Eve would think of:

> This institution,
> perhaps one should say enterprise
> out of respect for which
> one says one need not change one's mind
> about a thing one has believed in,
> requiring public promises
> of one's intention
> to fulfill a private obligation;

she notes wryly:

> Psychology which explains everything
> explains nothing,
> and we are still in doubt.

Her description of the male's encounter with marriage and his reaction is delightful, ironically commenting by implication upon the elaborate "scientific" apparatus with which a scientific age attempts to explain a very simple phenomenon:

> Unnerved by the nightingale
> and dazzled by the apple,
> impelled by "the illusion of a fire
> effectual to extinguish fire,"
> compared with which
> the shining of the earth
> is but deformity—a fire
> "as high as deep
> as bright as broad
> as long as life itself,"
> he stumbles over marriage,
> "a very trivial event indeed"

> to have destroyed the attitude
> in which he stood—
> the ease of a philosopher
> unfathered by a woman.

A single line can hold a penetrating observation, as in "Virginia Britannia"—

> Priorities were cradled in this region, not
> noted for humility;

or in "The Bear and the Garden-Lover," from *The Fables of La Fontaine*—

> Intimates should be feared who lack perspicacity;
> Choose wisdom, even in an enemy.

which can provoke a smile, even while the reader acknowledges its truth. Like Chaucer, whom she greatly admires, Marianne Moore reserves her indignation for moments when it is appropriate—the "pedantic literalist" is "marked for destruction," and William Blake's "tigers of wrath" are loosed to castigate the futility of war. Even in her remarkable anti-war poem "In Distrust of Merits," however, there is a concluding note of hope:

> If these great patient
> dyings—all these agonies
> and wound bearings and bloodshed—
> can teach us how to live, these
> dyings were not wasted.

But, though her poetry partakes of the general ethos of the eighteenth century, there is no similarity whatever in form. Nor is it derivative from any other source. A Moore poem is uniquely, unmistakably Moore. She firmly disparages a theory recently advanced, that her poems are planned deliberately to fit into a pre-arranged syllabic count—"*What* an idea!" she protests vigorously, her blue eyes sparking.[31] When her work was first published, Ezra Pound remarked that she must have been reading Laforgue and the French symbolists; actually she read them for the first time in the 1950's. She received no inspiration from the Imagist movement—"I wondered why anyone would adopt that term" [32]—nor from Amy Lowell's polyphonic prose.

Perhaps the poet whose approach most resembles hers is Gerard Manley Hopkins. As in his "sprung rhythm," the rhythm of normal speech provides her metrical pattern. "A felicitous phrase springs to mind—a word or two, say—simultaneous usually with some thought or object of equal attractiveness." [33] From that stage, it is a matter of arranging words in the most effective sequence—"proper words in proper places," as Jonathan Swift defines style. "Words cluster like chromosomes," Marianne Moore explains, "determining the procedure . . . if the phrases recur in too incoherent an architecture—as print—I notice that the words as a tune do not sound right." [34]

The key word is *sound*. T. S. Eliot has said of her, "What is certain is that Miss Moore's poems always read very well aloud;" [35] she writes for the ear, as well as for the eye. Her "passion for rhythm and accent" as well as for "architecture," leads her to eschew capitals at the beginning of the line unless she is beginning a new sentence, frequently to avoid titles— "Titles are chaff"—to use a minimum of connectives, and to pare and prune language down—to make an appropriate analogy, considering her love of things mechanical—to the steel beams of the poem. "Omissions," she says, "are not accidents."

At the same time, her poetry frequently reveals the influence of both Biblical and classical rhetoric. In "His Shield," which is a comment on pseudo-humility, adjective is piled upon adjective to heighten the ironic impact of the final word:

> Become dinosaur
> skulled, quilled, or salamander-wooled, more ironshod
> and javelin-dressed than a hedgehog battalion of steel, but be
> dull.

Sometimes there is a Ciceronian periodic sentence:

> Where the ground is sour; where there are
> weeds of beanstalk height,

snakes' hypodermic teeth, or
the wind brings the "scarebabe voice"
from the neglected new set
with the semi-precious cat's eyes of the owl—
awake, asleep, "raised ears extended to fine points," and so
on—love won't grow.

And occasionally the two are brilliantly combined, with the startling addition of James Joyce:

Love in America?
Whatever it is, it's a passion—
a benign dementia that should be
engulfing America, fed in a way
the opposite of the way
in which the Minotaur was fed.

It's a Midas of tenderness;
      from the heart;
nothing else. From one with ability
to bear being misunderstood—
         take blame, with "nobility
         that is action," identifying itself with
         pioneer unperfunctoriness

without brazenness or
bigness of overgrown
undergrown shallowness.
Whatever it is, let it be without
affectation.

Yes, yes, yes, *yes*.

But no matter how complex the sentence may be, there is never a loss or diminution of sense: "There is something attractive about a mind/ that moves in a straight line." Nor does the poet's insistence upon clarity and precision imply an obsession with the obvious. A Moore poem is subtle, demanding careful reading—sometimes several readings—but it is never obscure. "We are not daft about the meaning," she writes in

22 *Ibid.*

23 "A Burning Desire to Be Explicit," *Tell Me, Tell Me.*

24 "Profit Is a Dead Weight," *Tell Me, Tell Me.*

25 Foreword, *A Marianne Moore Reader.*

26 "Subject, Predicate, Object."

27 "Profit Is a Dead Weight."

28 Letter to author.

29 Foreword, *A Marianne Moore Reader.*

30 "Profit Is a Dead Weight."

31 See *Times Literary Supplement*, May 30th, 1968. Miss Moore's comment made to author.

32 "Interview with Donald Hall."

33 *Ibid.*

34 *Ibid.*

35 *The Dial*, December, 1923.

36 "Subject, Predicate, Object."

37 *Ibid.*

38 Conversation with author.

39 "Interview with Donald Hall."

40 *The Dial*, December, 1923.

"Picking and Choosing," in gentle rebuke to the symbol hunters, "but this familiarity with wrong meanings puzzles one."

"Form is synonymous with content—must be. . . ." [36] And the content of a Moore poem read once, read twice—innumerable times—fascinates. If it juxtaposes salamanders and hedgehogs, bronze dromios and peacocks, eagle's down and beaver's skin, church spires, bridges, baseball teams, china ornaments, race horses, elephants and poetry, it is always with *controlled* abandon. As elements of the life which the poet reflects, all these are interesting and important to her, but,

> . . . when dragged into prominence by half
> poets, the result is not poetry. . . .

Every aspect of a poem must be directed to the single end of "achieving a likeness of the thing visualized." [37] If one of the poet's gifts is the art of seeing connection between unconnectables, Marianne Moore not only possesses it, she revels in it. For, despite the severity of her style, she is passionately involved in her—our—world: "one detects creative power by its capacity to conquer one's detachment." With the humility of the great, she realizes that power within herself, but at the same time she realizes its dangers:

> Tell me, tell me
> where might be a refuge for me
> from egocentricity
> and its propensity to bisect,
> mis-state, misunderstand
> and obliterate continuity.

This she writes in the title poem of her latest volume, and, again, in "In Distrust of Merits," she acknowledges that:

> there never was a war that was
> not inward; I must
> fight till I have conquered in myself what
> causes war, but I would not believe it.

That Marianne Moore herself needs such a reminder is doubtful, but we can be grateful to her for reminding those countless numbers of us who do.

Asked what makes a poet, her favorite answer is, "Observation, research, and a great love for the thing." [38] It is the "love for the thing" that, in the final analysis, is the ultimate communication of a Marianne Moore poem, and of Marianne Moore herself. "Poetry is the Mogul's dream: to be intensively toiling at what is a pleasure," she wrote in a sparkling essay, entitled "Subject, Predicate, Object," and she emplifies that statement in her poem "Baseball and Writing," in terms that the Saturday afternoon television viewer can understand completely:

> "Yes,
> it's work; I want you to bear down,
>   but enjoy it
>   while you're doing it."

Although she admits freely to the difficulties that the worker with words encounters, the joy in the work transcends them; and in the finished, perfected poem, the difficulties do not appear and the joy remains, plus one other quality—integrity. In a world where moral values are shifting, and standards are constantly challenged, Marianne Moore stands firm for courage, honor, and an heroic attitude towards all life sends.

> Must a man be good to write good poems? The villains in Shakespeare are not illiterate, are they? But rectitude *has* a ring that is implicative, I would say. And with *no* integrity, a man is not likely to write the kind of book I read.[39]

Nor, it might be added, write the kind of poetry that she writes. If as T. S. Eliot has said, "one never forgets that it is written by a woman," one must also agree with him that "one never thinks of this particularity as anything but a positive virtue." [40] She does not preach; she does not even wear the prophet's cloak, unless it be, perhaps, an invisible one. But her penetrating, compassionate eyes can pierce chaos to the grand design be-

neath, and find good there; and with magnificent a lovingly—authoritatively—bids us be aware of that And, just as the twentieth century is now belatedly d the relevance of the vision of poets of ages past, later may wonder why we have been so blind to Marianne M

Footnotes

All poems from *The Complete Poems of Marianne M* millan Co./Viking Press, 1967.

The two selections from Miss Moore's translation of La Fon *The Fables of La Fontaine*, Viking Press, 1954.

The 1935 version of "Poetry" is quoted with the poet permission, at the author's special request.

[1] Marianne Moore, "Subject, Predicate, Object," *Tell Me, Tell Me* (Viking Press, 1966), 46.

[2] Conversation with author.

[3] *Newsweek*, November 25, 1968.

[4] "Subject, Predicate, Object."

[5] *Selected Poems* (Macmillan, 1935), postscript.

[6] "Interview with Donald Hall," reprinted in *A Marianne Moore Reader* (Viking, 1965).

[7] Conversation with author.

[8] "M. Carey Thomas of Bryn Mawr," reprinted in *A Marianne Moore Reader*.

[9] "If I Were Sixteen Today," reprinted in *A Marianne Moore Reader*.

[10] *Ibid.*

[11] Bryn Mawr College *Alumnae Bulletin*, 1966–7, No. 3.

[12] Conversation with

[13] Harriet Monroe, *Life* (Macmillan, 1938),

[14] "Interview with Hall."

[15] William Carlos *The Autobiography of Carlos Williams* (Rando: 1948), 146.

[16] Ezra Pound's com tation to author from Mi Eliot quotation from *T* December, 1923.

[17] "Interview with Hall."

[18] *Ibid.*

[19] "Brooklyn from Hill," reprinted in *A* *Moore Reader*.

[20] "If I Were Sixteen

[21] "Interview with Hall."

Poems

The Steeplejack

Revised 1961

Dürer would have seen a reason for living
    in a town like this, with eight stranded whales
to look at; with the sweet sea air coming into your house
on a fine day, from water etched
    with waves as formal as the scales
on a fish.

One by one in two's and three's, the seagulls keep
    flying back and forth over the town clock,
or sailing around the lighthouse without moving their
                      wings—
rising steadily with a slight
    quiver of the body—or flock
mewing where

a sea the purple of the peacock's neck is
    paled to greenish azure as Dürer changed
the pine green of the Tyrol to peacock blue and guinea
gray. You can see a twenty-five-
    pound lobster; and fish nets arranged
to dry. The

whirlwind fife-and-drum of the storm bends the salt
    marsh grass, disturbs stars in the sky and the
star on the steeple; it is a privilege to see so
much confusion. Disguised by what
    might seem the opposite, the sea-
side flowers and

trees are favored by the fog so that you have
        the tropics at first hand: the trumpet vine,
foxglove, giant snapdragon, a salpiglossis that has
spots and stripes; morning-glories, gourds,
        or moon-vines trained on fishing twine
at the back door:

cattails, flags, blueberries and spiderwort,
        striped grass, lichens, sunflowers, asters, daisies—
yellow and crab-claw ragged sailors with green bracts—
                        toad-plant,
petunias, ferns; pink lilies, blue
        ones, tigers; poppies; black sweet-peas.
The climate

is not right for the banyan, frangipani, or
        jack-fruit trees; or for exotic serpent
life. Ring lizard and snakeskin for the foot, if you see fit;
but here they've cats, not cobras to
        keep down the rats. The diffident
little newt

with white pin-dots on black horizontal-spaced-
        out bands lives here; yet there is nothing that
ambition can buy or take away. The college student
named Ambrose sits on the hillside
        with his not-native books and hat
and sees boats

at sea progress white and rigid as if in
        a groove. Liking an elegance of which
the source is not bravado, he knows by heart the antique
sugar-bowl shaped summerhouse of
        interlacing slats, and the pitch
of the church

spire, not true, from which a man in scarlet lets
        down a rope as a spider spins a thread;

he might be part of a novel, but on the sidewalk a
sign says C.J. Poole, Steeple Jack,
        in black and white; and one in red
and white says

Danger. The church portico has four fluted
        columns, each a single piece of stone, made
modester by whitewash. This would be a fit haven for
waifs, children, animals, prisoners
        and presidents who have repaid
sin-driven

senators by not thinking about them. The
        place has a schoolhouse, a post-office in a
store, fish-houses, hen-houses, a three-masted
        schooner on
the stocks. The hero, the student,
        the steeple jack, each in his way,
is at home.

It could not be dangerous to be living
        in a town like this, of simple people,
who have a steeple-jack placing danger signs by the church
while he is gilding the solid-
        pointed star, which on a steeple
stands for hope.

No Swan so Fine

"No water so still as the
        dead fountains of Versailles." No swan,
with swart blind look askance
and gondoliering legs, so fine
        as the chintz china one with fawn-
brown eyes and toothed gold
collar on to show whose bird it was.

Lodged in the Louis Fifteenth
      candelabrum-tree of cockscomb-
tinted buttons, dahlias,
sea urchins, and everlastings,
      it perches on the branching foam
of polished sculptured
flowers—at ease and tall. The king is dead.

The Buffalo

      Black in blazonry means
prudence; and niger, unpropitious. Might
hematite—
      black, compactly incurved horns on bison
            have significance? The
      soot-brown tail-tuft on
            a kind of lion

      tail; what would that express?
And John Steuart Curry's Ajax pulling
grass—no ring
      in his nose—two birds standing on the back?

            .   .   .   .   .   .
            The modern
ox does not look like the Augsburg ox's
portrait. Yes,
      the great extinct wild aurochs was a beast
            to paint, with stripe and six-
      foot horn spread—decreased
            to Siamese-cat

      brown Swiss size or zebu-
shape, with white plush dewlap and warm-blooded
hump; to red-
      skinned Hereford or to piebald Holstein. Yet
            some would say the sparse-haired

buffalo has met
　　human notions best

　　unlike the elephant,
both jewel and jeweller in the hairs
that he wears—
　　　　no white-nosed Vermont ox yoked with its twin
　　　　　to haul the maple sap,
　　　　up to their knees in
　　　　　　snow; no freakishly

　　　　over-drove ox drawn by
Rowlandson, but the Indian buffalo,
albino-
　　　　footed, standing in a mud lake with a
　　　　　day's work to do. No white
　　　　Christian heathen, way-
　　　　　　laid by the Buddha,

　　　　serves him so well as the
buffalo—as mettlesome as if check-
reined—free neck
　　　　stretching out, and snake tail in a half-twist
　　　　　on the flank; nor will so
　　　　cheerfully assist
　　　　　　the Sage sitting with

　　　　feet at the same side, to
dismount at the shrine; nor are there any
ivory
　　　　tusks, like those two horns which when a tiger
　　　　　coughs, are lowered fiercely
　　　　and convert the fur
　　　　　　to harmless rubbish.

　　　　The Indian buffalo,
led by bare-leggèd herd-boys to a hay
hut where they
　　　　stable it, need not fear comparison

with bison, with the twins,
indeed with any
of ox ancestry.

To a Giraffe

If it is unpermissible, in fact fatal
to be personal and undesirable

to be literal—detrimental as well
if the eye is not innocent—does it mean that

one can live only on top leaves that are small
reachable only by a beast that is tall?—

of which the giraffe is the best example—
the unconversational animal.

When plagued by the psychological,
a creature can be unbearable

that could have been irresistible;
or to be exact, exceptional

since less conversational
than some emotionally-tied-in-knots animal.

After all
consolations of the metaphysical
can be profound. In Homer, existence

is flawed; transcendence, conditional;
"the journey from sin to redemption, perpetual."

O To Be a Dragon

If I, like Solomon, . . .
could have my wish—

my wish . . . O to be a dragon,
a symbol of the power of Heaven—of silkworm
size or immense; at times invisible.
   Felicitous phenomenon!

Silence

My father used to say,
"Superior people never make long visits,
have to be shown Longfellow's grave
or the glass flowers at Harvard.
Self-reliant like the cat—
that takes its prey to privacy,
the mouse's limp tail hanging like a shoelace from its
                     mouth—
they sometimes enjoy solitude,
and can be robbed of speech
by speech which has delighted them.
The deepest feeling always shows itself in silence;
not in silence, but restraint."
Nor was he insincere in saying, "Make my house your
                     inn."
Inns are not residences.

Injudicious Gardening

If yellow token infidelity,
   I am an infidel.
      I could not bear a yellow rose ill will
        because books said that yellow boded ill,
   white promised well.

However, your particular possession,
   the sense of privacy,

indeed might deprecate
offended ears, and need not tolerate
effrontery.

The Past Is Present

If external action is effete
    and rhyme is outmoded,
        I shall revert to you,
Habakkuk, as when in a Bible class
    the teacher was speaking of unrhymed verse.
He said—and I think I repeat his exact words—
    "Hebrew poetry is prose
    with a sort of heightened consciousness." Ecstasy
        affords
    the occasion and expendiency determines the
        form.

Picking and Choosing

Literature is a phase of life. If one is afraid of it,
the situation is irremediable; if one approaches it
        familiarly,
what one says of it is worthless.
The opaque allusion, the simulated flight upward,
accomplishes nothing. Why cloud the fact
that Shaw is self-conscious in the field of sentiment
but is otherwise rewarding; that James
is all that has been said of him. It is not Hardy the
        novelist
and Hardy the poet, but one man interperting life as
        emotion.
The critic should know what he likes:
Gordon Craig with his "this is I" and "this is mine,"

with his three wise men, his "sad French greens," and
        his "Chinese cherry"—
Gordon Craig so inclinational and unashamed—a critic.
And Burke is a psychologist, of acute racoon-like
        curiosity.
Summa diligentia; to the humbug whose name is so
        amusing—
very young and very rushed—Caesar crossed the Alps
on the top of a *"diligence"*!
We are not daft about the meaning,
but this familiarity with wrong meanings puzzles one.
Humming-bug, the candles are not wired for elec-
        tricity.
Small dog, going over the lawn nipping the linen
        and saying
that you have a badger—remember Xenophon;
only rudimentary behavior is necessary to put us
        on the scent.
"A right good salvo of barks," a few strong wrinkles
        puckering
    the skin between the ears, is all we ask.

I May, I Might, I Must

If you will tell me why the fen
appears impassable, I then
will tell you why I think that I
can get across it if I try.

Like a Bulwark

Affirmed. Pent by power that holds it fast—
a paradox. Pent. Hard pressed,
    you take the blame and are inviolate.

Abased at last?
Not the tempest-tossed.
Compressed; firmed by the thrust of the blast
till compact, like a bulwark against fate;
lead-saluted,
saluted by lead?
As though flying Old Glory full mast.

The Pot of Clay and the Pot of Iron

A pot of iron's proposal
That a clay pot fare afield,
Met with a prompt refusal:
"Any joy that journeys yield
Is afforded by our warm hearth;
Brittle pots of breakable earth
Are inured to sacrifice,
Since jostles are far from wise:
I might be crushed by a blow;
But don't feel that you should not go.
Since iron is accustomed to strain,
No reason why you should remain."
Then the other turned arguer
And said, "As for shocks you'd incur,
Or objects you saw to fear,
If you felt you'd come too near,
I'd expose myself instead
And you'd not be buffeted."
The clay pot was satisfied
So they fared forth side by side—
The iron, and the clay one protected,
Each on three legs as pots are constructed.
Clipper-clap-clip they tried their luck
And then at each jolt conflicted
If even pebbles were struck.

The clay pot suffered, in less than fifty paces, the worst that could
        befall—
Left by the iron pot in fagments so minute you could not count
        them all
    And with only himself to blame.
Take as an equal a person who is not,
    And your fate may be the same
    As that of the earthen pot.

From *The Fables of La Fontaine*

The Serpent and the File

A snake, so they say, lived near a watchmaker
(Rather unfortunate for a man with just that work);
The serpent glided in for something to stay hunger.
        However, his flickering fork
Could find nothing but a file to endanger.
Kindly, with anything but an injured air,
    The file said, "Poor worm, aren't you courting
            despair?
        A great fool, little snake, although small.
        By the time my filings could yield
        The fourth of an obol in all,
        You would break your two teeth in.
        Only Time's tooth wears me thin."

Now this is meant for you, vapid second-rate minds,
Good-for-nothings who try to harm worth of all
            kinds.
        Your gnashed teeth imply nothing profound.
Do you think that you could leave a toothmark
        On any masterwork?
Bite steel or burnished brass or dent the diamond?

From *The Fables of La Fontaine*

Granite and Steel

Enfranchising cable, silvered by the sea,
　of woven wire, grayed by the mist,
　and Liberty dominate the Bay—
　her feet as one on shattered chains,
　once whole links wrought by Tyranny.

　Caged Circe of steel and stone,
　her parent German ingenuity.
　"O catenary curve" from tower to pier,
　implacable enemy of the mind's deformity,
　of man's uncompunctious greed,
　his crass love of crass priority
　　　just recently
　obstructing acquiescent feet
　about to step ashore when darkness fell
　　　without a cause,
　as if probity had not joined our cities
　　　in the sea.

　"O path amid the stars
　crossed by the seagull's wing!"
　"O radiance that doth inherit me!"
　—affirming inter-acting harmony!

　Untried expedient, untried; then tried;
　way out; way in; romantic passageway
　first seen by the eye of the mind,
　then by the eye. O steel! O stone!
　Climactic ornament, double rainbow,
　as if invented by French perspicacity,
　　　John Roebling's monument,
　　　German tenacity's also;
　　　composite span—an actuality.

In Distrust of Merits

Strengthened to live, strengthened to die for
    medals and positioned victories?
They're fighting, fighting, fighting the blind
    man who thinks he sees—
who cannot see that the enslaver is
enslaved; the hater, harmed. O shining O
        firm star, O tumultuous
            ocean lashed till small things go
        as they will, the mountainous
            wave makes us who look, know

depth. Lost at sea before they fought! O
        star of David, star of Bethlehem,
O black imperial lion
        of the Lord—emblem
of a risen world—be joined at last, be
joined. There is hate's crown beneath which all is
        death; there's love's without which none
            is king; the blessed deeds bless
        the halo. As contagion
            of sickness makes sickness,

contagion of trust can make trust. They're
        fighting in deserts and caves, one by
one, in battalions and squadrons;
        they're fighting that I
may yet recover from the disease, My
Self; some have it lightly; some will die. "Man's
        wolf to man" and we devour
            ourselves. The enemy could not
        have made a greater breach in our
            defenses. One pilot-

ing a blind man can escape him, but
    Job disheartened by false comfort knew
that nothing can be so defeating
    as a blind man who
can see. O alive who are dead, who are
proud not to see, O small dust of the earth
      that walks so arrogantly,
          trust begets power and faith is
      an affectionate thing. We
      vow, we make this promise

to the fighting—it's a promise—"We'll
    never hate black, white, red, yellow, Jew,
Gentile, Untouchable." We are
    not competent to
make our vows. With set jaw they are fighting,
fighting, fighting—some we love whom we know,
      some we love but know not—that
        hearts may feel and be not numb.
    It cures me; or am I what
    I can't believe in? Some

in snow, some on crags, some in quicksands,
    little by little, much by much, they
are fighting fighting fighting that where
    there was death there may
be life. "When a man is prey to anger,
he is moved by outside things; when he holds
      his ground in patience patience
      patience, that is action
    or beauty," the soldier's defense
    and hardest armor for

the fight. The world's an orphans' home. Shall
    we never have peace without sorrow?
without pleas of the dying for
    help that won't come? O

quiet form upon the dust, I cannot
look and yet I must. If these great patient
   dyings—all these agonies
     and wound-bearings and bloodshed—
   can teach us how to live, these
    dyings were not wasted.

  Hate-hardened heart, O heart of iron,
    iron is iron till it is rust.
There never was a war that was
    not inward; I must
fight till I have conquered in myself what
causes war, but I would not believe it.
    I inwardly did nothing.
     O Iscariot-like crime!
    Beauty is everlasting
     and dust is for a time.

Poetry, 1935

I too, dislike it: there are things that are important beyond all
               this fiddle.
Reading it, however, with a perfect contempt for it, one
              discovers in
it after all, a place for the genuine.
    Hands that can grasp, eyes
      that can dilate, hair that can rise
       if it must, these things are important not because a

high—sounding interpretation can be put upon them but
              because they are
useful. When they become so derivative as to become
              unintelligible,
the same thing may be said for all of us, that we
    do not admire what

we cannot understand: the bat
holding on upside down or in quest of something to

eat, elephants pushing, a wild horse taking a roll, a tireless wolf
under
a tree, the immovable critic twitching his skin like a horse
that feels a flea, the base-
ball fan, the statistician—
nor is it valid
to discriminate gainst "business documents and

school-books"; all these phenomena are important. One must
make a distinction
however: when dragged into prominence by half poets, the
result is not poetry,
nor until the poets among us can be
"literalists of the imagination"—above
insolence and triviality and can present

for inspection, "imaginary gardens with real toads in them,"
shall we have
it. In the meantime, if you demand on the one hand,
the raw material of poetry in
all its rawness and
that which is on the other hand
genuine, you are interested in poetry.

Poetry—1967

I, too, dislike it.
Reading it, however, with a perfect contempt for it, one
discovers in
it, after all, a place for the genuine.

The Student

"In America," began
the lecturer, "everyone must have a
degree. The French do not think that
all can have it, they don't say everyone
    must go to college." We
incline to feel
    that although it may be unnecessary

to know fifteen languages,
one degree is not too much. With us, a
school—like the singing tree of which
the leaves were mouths singing in concert—
    is both a tree of knowledge
and of liberty—
    seen in the unanimity of college

mottoes, *Lux et veritas,*
Christo et ecclesiae, Sapient
felici. It may be that we
have not knowledge, just opinions, that we
    are undergraduates,
not students; we know
    we have been told with smiles, by expatriates

of whom we had asked "When will
your experiment be finished?" "Science
is never finished." Secluded
from domestic strife, Jack Bookworm led a
    college life, says Goldsmith;
and here also as
    in France or Oxford, study is beset with

dangers,—with bookworms, mildews,
and complaisancies. But someone in New

England has known enough to say
the student is patience personified,
   is a variety
of hero, "patient
   of neglect and of reproach"—who can "hold by

himself." You can't beat hens to
make them lay. Wolf's wool is the best of wool,
but it cannot be sheared because
the wolf will not comply. With knowledge as
   with the wolf's surliness,
the student studies
   voluntarily, refusing to be less

than individual. He
"gives his opinion and then rests on it";
he renders service when there is
no reward, and is too reclusive for
   some things to seem to touch
him, not because he
   has no feeling, but because he has so much.

What Are Years?

   What is our innocence,
what is our guilt? All are
   naked, none is safe. And whence
is courage: the unanswered question,
   the resolute doubt—
dumbly calling, deafly listening—that
in misfortune, even death,
      encourages others
      and in its defeat, stirs

   the soul to be strong? He
sees deep and is glad, who

accedes to mortality
and in his imprisonment rises
upon himself as
the sea in a chasm, struggling to be
free and unable to be,
     in its surrendering
     finds its continuing.

So he who strongly feels,
behaves. The very bird,
     grown taller as he sings, steels
his form straight up. Though he is captive,
his mighty singing
says, satisfaction is a lowly
thing, how pure a thing is joy.
     this is mortality,
     this is eternity.

Index

232   * *IMAGINARY GARDENS* *

*R*OSEMARY SPRAGUE, whose highly acclaimed *Red Lion Gold Dragon: A Novel of the Norman Conquest* was published in 1966 by Chilton Book Company, was born in New York. She moved to Cleveland when she was about a year old. She admits that she was not overly fond of school. Her parents were aware of this, although they never let her know that they knew until she was in college. She learned to read before she entered the first grade, a discovery which surprised her father and mother as greatly as it annoyed the teacher!

With Cornelia Otis Skinner, she feels she shares the honor of being the most innocent freshman ever to enter Bryn Mawr College. There, she majored in English, took all the languages and history she could, and was an active member of the Dramatic Society, choir, and glee club.

Following her graduation from Bryn Mawr, she spent a year in New York studying acting with the late Frances Robinson-Duff. Then she entered graduate school at Western Reserve University, where she took her M.A., and was a Fellow-in-English during her last two years' work on her Ph.D. Since receiving her doctorate, she studied at the Shakespeare Institute at Stratford-on-Avon, England, and the University of London. She has been a delegate to the Conference on English Literature at Oxford University in England and to the Conférence sur des Auteurs Français at Brussels. She was also a member of the first School of Letters (New Criticism) at Kenyon College.

In 1962 she attended the Shakespeare Seminar at Stratford, Ontario, and delivered a lecture there on "The Men Who Were Not Shakespeare." She has also lectured extensively on children's literature; on Robert Browning; and on Queen Elizabeth I at the Thomas More Institute of the University of Montreal.

She has taught at Western Reserve University; Fenn College, Cleveland, Ohio; The Cleveland Institute of Art; and was director of dramatics at Notre Dame College, South Euclid, Ohio, where she staged the North American premiere of Paul Claudel's *The Satin Slipper*. She is now professor of English at Longwood College, Farmville, Virginia, the oldest women's college in the United States, where she teaches her two specialties, the Victorians and Chaucer. In her spare time, she plays the piano, experiments with gourmet cooking, continues to read incessantly, and goes to the theater.

Miss Sprague has carved a distinguished career for herself as the author of many historical novels for young adults. *Northward to Albion* was the first and was followed by *A Kingdom to Win*, and *Heroes of the White Shield*. *Heir of Kiloran* grew out of her love of the theater and the *commedia del' arte*, in addition to her fascination with the outcome of the intrigues surrounding Mary Stuart. It was named one of the 100 Best Books of 1956 by *The New York Times Book Review*. This was followed by such books as *Conquerors of Time, Dance for a Diamond Star*—concerning Maria de Camargo, the eighteenth-century ballerina—and *The Jade Pagoda*, set in Salem, Massachusetts, in the days of the China trade. In 1965, Chilton published her biography of Browning: *Forever in Joy: The Life of Robert Browning*. Her biography of George Eliot was published in 1968.

Rosemary Sprague has recently edited *Poems of Robert Browning*.